Sebastian, Have fun! Grampa Everett March 30, 2021

THE

EVERYTHING®

KIDS' COOKBOOK

Updated Edition

90+ Easy Recipes You'll Love to Make—and Eat!

Sandra K. Nissenberg, MS, RD

ADAMS MEDIA

New York London Toronto Sydney New Delhi

Aadamsmedia

Adams Media
An Imprint of Simon & Schuster, Inc.
57 Littlefield Street
Avon, Massachusetts 02322

Copyright © 2002, 2008, 2020 by Simon & Schuster, Inc.

All rights reserved, including the right to reproduce this book or portions thereof in any form whatsoever. For information address Adams Media Subsidiary Rights Department, 1230 Avenue of the Americas, New York, NY 10020.

An Everything® Series Book.
Everything® and everything.com® are registered trademarks of Simon & Schuster, Inc.

This Adams Media trade paperback edition October 2020

ADAMS MEDIA and colophon are trademarks of Simon & Schuster.

For information about special discounts for bulk purchases, please contact Simon & Schuster Special Sales at 1-866-506-1949 or business@simonandschuster.com.

The Simon & Schuster Speakers Bureau can bring authors to your live event. For more information or to book an event contact the Simon & Schuster Speakers Bureau at 1-866-248-3049 or visit our website at www.simonspeakers.com.

Interior design by Erin Alexander
Photographs by Kelly Jaggers
Illustrations by Jim Steck

Manufactured in the United States of America

Printed by LSC Communications, Willard, OH, U.S.A.
10   9   8   7   6   5   4   3   2   1
September 2020

ISBN 978-1-5072-1400-8
ISBN 978-1-5072-1401-5 (ebook)

Many of the designations used by manufacturers and sellers to distinguish their products are claimed as trademarks. Where those designations appear in this book and Simon & Schuster, Inc., was aware of a trademark claim, the designations have been printed with initial capital letters.

Always follow safety and commonsense cooking protocols while using kitchen utensils, operating ovens and stoves, and handling uncooked food. Children should always be supervised by an adult.

Contents

A Note to Parents and Guardians

Kids love to have fun, get messy, and be creative. And it's a known fact, when kids play with various foods—touch them and smell them—it's more likely they will eat them. Kids having fun, cooking, and eating better—it's a "win-win" for the whole family!

When I first started writing kids' cookbooks, my kids were young. They enjoyed everything about being with me in the kitchen. They played with my pots and pans, my wooden spoons, and even my plastic containers. Whenever they asked to help, I found them something to do, instead of sending them out of the kitchen. Whether it was washing and tearing lettuce for a salad, stirring up a batter, setting the table, or sampling a recipe—there was something I could find to keep them busy. Now that they are older, they have a better understanding of the ins and outs of meal planning, food preparation, and, of course, nutrition. As a registered dietitian, I could not be prouder of them. Our time together in the kitchen provided them with a strong foundation for being independent adults, and I know that they will teach their future families about the importance of cooking and eating together as well.

We have seen a strong interest in kids' nutrition over the years and the need to start teaching early so kids will enjoy happy, healthy lives as they get older. If we can get children interested in choosing good foods and understanding how it makes them feel, they will be off to the best start life has to offer.

This updated edition of *The Everything® Kids' Cookbook* includes current information that is relevant to today's kids. We've added some new recipes and improved others, but the old favorites that stand the test of time are still here. And for the first time, nutrition facts are available for each recipe to help you understand what's in the foods you and your family choose. The book continues to incorporate fun too. You'll still find games, puzzles, and fun food trivia to make you smile and your days brighter.

Kids (and adults) will continue to enjoy everything *The Everything® Kids' Cookbook, Updated Edition* has to offer. Remember, the most important lesson of all is to build strong memories with your families that last a lifetime.

Happy, healthy eating to you and your family.
Sandy Nissenberg

Chapter 1

LET'S GET COOKING

Welcome to the creative—and delicious—world of cooking! Whether you've been helping make dinner every night, tried making cookies or brownies with your friends, or just enjoyed being in the kitchen where all the magic happens—this book is for you! In these pages, you'll find more than ninety recipes you can make for breakfast, lunch, dinner, dessert, and snacks. Learn how to make eggs any way you like them, put together a quick after-school snack for yourself, or impress your family with homemade macaroni and cheese that doesn't come from a box!

TASTY TUNA MELTS

Tuna melts are delicious for lunch or as an afternoon snack. For a fun change, bake a potato in the microwave, top it with tuna and cheese, and bake it. You will have a Tuna Melt Potato!

SERVES 4 **3**

2 English muffins or bagels, split in half

1 (5-ounce) can chunk tuna in water

1½ tablespoons mayonnaise **4**

¼ cup shredded Cheddar cheese

1. Preheat the oven to 350°F. **5**
2. Place English muffin or bagel halves on a baking sheet.
3. Use a can opener to open the tuna can (be careful of sharp edges!), then dump the tuna into a colander. Press down lightly on the tuna to remove most of the water. **6**
4. Put the tuna in a medium bowl and use a wooden spoon or fork to break it up into small pieces.
5. Add the mayonnaise to the tuna and mix well.
6. Top each English muffin or bagel half with the tuna mixture, then with cheese.
7. Bake for 5-8 minutes until the cheese is melted. Use pot holders to remove the baking sheet from the oven. Serve warm.

8 PER SERVING

Calories: 150 | Fat: 6g | Sodium: 300mg | Carbohydrates: 13g | Fiber: 0g | Sugar: 1g | Protein: 11g

Each recipe is rated Easy, Medium, or Hard. This will help you to decide whether you can try a recipe by yourself or ask a grownup for help. The more you cook, the more you'll find that cooking is really simple—all you need to do is follow directions. The recipes tell you all you need to know!

The best things about cooking are that you can be creative, experiment, and share what you make. Like any activity that involves experimentation, there are tools, terms, and things to know. The next few sections aren't as exciting as making Cheesy Quesadillas (Chapter 3) or Banana Split Ice Cream Pie (Chapter 7), but they are pretty important. Otherwise, how will you know whether to bake or boil? Slice or mash?

Read this chapter with your parents or the adult who will be helping you in the kitchen. The recipes are written for you, but it's important for all the cooks to know what's going on.

Reading Recipes

A recipe is a set of instructions for making a particular food. It is important to read the recipe carefully so you understand how to make the food and what ingredients you will need to make it. Recipes in this book include:

1 Level of difficulty
2 Tools of the trade
3 Quantity *(or number of servings)* that the recipe makes
4 An ingredient list
5 Oven temperature *(if necessary)*
6 Easy-to-understand instructions
7 Baking or cooking times
8 Nutritional information

Read through the entire recipe. Make sure you have everything you need and you have enough time to make it. Get all the ingredients and tools ready before getting started.

Important Safety Tips and Kitchen Rules

Safety should be your number-one priority when working and cooking in the kitchen. Hot food or pans, boiling water, and sharp knives can all be dangerous if you don't know how to handle them properly. Always check with an adult or parent before working in the kitchen, and be sure to review these handy safety tips and kitchen rules before starting:

- **Read the entire recipe before you begin.** Find out what ingredients and utensils you will need. You'll also want to know how long a recipe takes to prepare and how many people it will feed.

- *Make a shopping list of things you need.* Include items you will need to keep the kitchen well stocked (such as sugar, eggs, or milk). Some items you may have to buy, but you may have others in your house already.

- **Wash your hands with soap and water before touching food.** It is also important to wash your hands right after you handle raw meat, chicken, or fish before you start touching other things.

- *Tie back long hair, put on an apron, and pull up long sleeves.* Long hair and long sleeves can get in the way of your prepping and cooking. Putting on an apron helps keep your clothes clean. These are good habits to learn.

- **Start with a clean cooking area.** Otherwise, dirty dishes will be in your way, dirty counters will ruin your food, and other things on the counter or table (like mail) may get stained or splashed while you cook.

- *Don't overfill pots and pans.* If they overflow while you are cooking, you will definitely end up with a mess, and you might get splattered or splashed with hot liquids.

- *Know how to use the various appliances and utensils you will need.* If you need to, ask an adult to teach or remind you, especially if you are using anything with hot oil (like a wok) or sharp moving parts (like a blender or food processor).

- **Be careful with knives.** Learn how to hold them, wash them, and store them properly.

- *Put ingredients away when you have finished with them.* Also, be sure to wipe down, unplug, and turn off all appliances when you're done.

- **Wipe counters clean while working.** Put dirty dishes in the sink to keep them away from the clean ones.

- *Keep electric appliances away from water and the sink.* Also, try to keep the cords up on the counter so you don't trip or step on them by accident.

- **Always use pot holders or oven mitts to touch hot pans and dishes.** You may not realize how hot something is until you've touched it or picked it up, so it's always better to start out with your hands protected.

- *Know where to find things and where to put them away.* By keeping everything in its place, you will have a clean cooking area and you won't lose things.

- **Do only one job at a time.** Cooking requires planning and concentration—it's a lot like juggling! As you practice, you can do more and more, but in the beginning, just focus on one thing.

- *Get help.* Adults should supervise all your food preparation and cooking activities. It's important for you to learn how to work in a kitchen—and enjoy it!—but it's also important that you remember safety. Make sure an adult knows exactly what you are doing and will be able to give help if you need it.

The recipes in this book list the tools in advance so you know if you have everything you will need. The information about difficulty is pretty helpful for you too. Some recipes can go from Hard to Easy just by having an adult do the cutting with sharp knives—it's that simple!

Tools for Cooking

Proper tools and utensils are a must for preparing food. Let's take a look at some of the most common cooking utensils and equipment you can find in the kitchen...

 Baking pan—a square or rectangular pan (glass or metal) used for baking and cooking food in the oven

 Baking sheet (also called cookie sheet or sheet pan)—a flat metal sheet used for baking cookies or other nonrunny items

 Baking spatula—a utensil with a wide plastic or silicone blade used to fold foods together or scrape down batter from mixing bowls

 Blender—an electric appliance used for blending liquids and grinding food

 Can opener—a tool, either manual or electric, designed to open cans

 Casserole dish—a glass dish, usually a 1-quart or 2-quart size, used to make casseroles or baked goods in the oven

 Colander—a metal or plastic bowl with holes in it used to drain water or liquids from foods such as pasta or vegetables

 Cooling rack—a wire rack on which hot food is placed, allowing air to circulate all around the items

 Electric mixer—an electric appliance used for mixing ingredients (like cake batter) together

 Ice cream scoop—a plastic or metal tool, shaped like a big spoon, used to scoop ice cream from a carton

 Kitchen shears—scissors for the kitchen that can be used to cut herbs and other foods

 Knife and cutting board—a tool with a sharp blade and a handle used to slice or chop foods; a cutting board is made from wood or hard plastic and should be used when slicing or chopping ingredients

 Ladle—a large cup-shaped spoon with a long handle used to serve soup, stew, or chili

 Liquid measuring cup—a glass or plastic cup used to measure liquids, with various measurements printed along the side

 Measuring cups—plastic or metal cups in different sizes used to measure dry ingredients, like sugar or flour

 Measuring spoons—plastic or metal spoons in different sizes used to measure small amounts of both liquid and dry ingredients

Microwave oven—a small oven that heats food very quickly by cooking with electromagnetic waves (microwaves)

Mixing bowls—bowls (in various sizes) in which you mix ingredients together

Muffin tin—a metal or glass pan with small round cups used for baking muffins and cupcakes

Oven—a kitchen appliance for baking or broiling food

Parfait glass—a special glass used to serve parfaits; it usually has a wide mouth and a narrower bottom

Pastry brush—a small brush used to spread melted butter or sauces over food

Pizza cutter—a tool with a rolling cutter used to easily cut pizzas, doughs, or flatbreads

Plate—a flat dish used to serve food

Potato masher—a tool used to mash cooked potatoes—or anything soft—to make them smooth

Pot holders/oven mitts—pads or mittens used to hold hot pots, pans, baking sheets, and plates

Rolling pin—a wooden or plastic roller used to flatten an item such as dough for a piecrust

Saucepan—a pot with a projecting handle used for stovetop cooking

Serving spoon—a large spoon used to scoop out portions of food

Skillet—a pan used for frying, stir-frying, and sautéing food in hot fat or oil

Slotted spoon—a large spoon with holes in it to let liquid pass through

Stove—a kitchen appliance with gas or electric burners used for cooking food (also called a range or cooktop)

Toaster oven—a small oven that sits on the kitchen counter used to toast, bake, or broil a small amount of food

Tongs—a tool used to grasp, move, flip, and sear food, with two long arms joined at one end

Turning spatula—a utensil with a wide, thin blade that is used to lift, turn, and flip foods like eggs, cookies, and hamburgers

Whisk—a utensil used for mixing and stirring liquid ingredients, like eggs and milk, together

Wooden spoon—a big spoon made out of wood that is used for mixing and stirring just about any kind of food

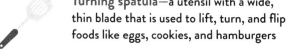
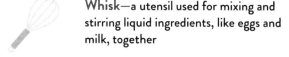
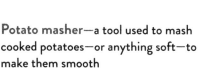

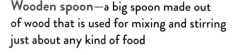

Cooking Terms

It can sometimes be confusing to understand all the words used to describe different ways to prepare and cook foods in a recipe. Here is a reference guide to help.

Bake—to cook something inside an oven

Batter—a mixture made from ingredients like sugar, eggs, flour, and water that is used to make cakes, cookies, and pancakes

Beat—to mix hard and thoroughly with a spoon, fork, whisk, or electric mixer

Blend—to mix foods together until smooth

Boil—to cook in a liquid until bubbles appear or until a liquid reaches its boiling point (water boils at 212°F/100°C)

Broil—to put food under the broiler part of the oven, where the heat source is on top of the food

Brown—to cook at low to medium heat until food turns brown

Chill—to refrigerate food until it is cold

Chop—to cut food into small pieces with a knife, blender, or food processor

Cool—to let food sit at room temperature until it is no longer hot

Cream—to mix ingredients like sugar, butter, and eggs together until they are smooth and creamy

Dice—to chop food into small, even-sized square pieces

Drain—to pour off a liquid in which the food has been cooked or stored

Drizzle—to sprinkle drops of liquid, like chocolate syrup or an icing, lightly over the top of something, like cookies or a cake

Fold—to gently combine ingredients together from top to bottom until they are just mixed together

Grate—to shred food into tiny pieces with a grater, blender, or food processor

Bake

Boil

Simmer

Stir-Fry

Crazy Cookbooks Use the Letter-Number Key to fill in the blanks.

1=A
2=E
3=I
4=O
5=U
6=V
7=W
8=Y

1000 P_ST_ D_SH_S, B_ M_CK _. R_N__
      1 1   3 2   8 1   1 4 28

Q__CK C__K_NG, B_ M_K_ R__ ____
5 3   44 3   8 3 2 4 2 7 1 6 2

__MM_ __G_T_BL_S, B_ BR_CK _'L__GH
85   8 62 2 1 2 8 4 4 2 3

M_X_C_N M__LS, B_ _UNT CH_L_D_
2 3 1 21 8 1 3 1 1

L_S_ ___GHT!, B_ C_L _. R__Z_
4 2 7 2 3 8 1 4 22 2

Grease—to rub a baking pan or a dish with butter, vegetable shortening, or oil (or spray it with nonstick cooking spray) so food cooked on it won't stick

Knead—to fold, press, and turn dough to make it the right consistency

Mash—to crush food, like cooked potatoes, into a soft mixture

Mince—to cut food into very small pieces

Mix—to stir two or more ingredients together until they are evenly combined

Preheat—to turn an oven on and let it heat up before putting the food inside

Purée—to mix in a blender or food processor until food is smooth and has the consistency of applesauce or a milkshake

Sauté—to cook food on the stovetop in a skillet with a little liquid or oil

Simmer—to cook over low heat while the food almost boils

Slice—to cut food into even-sized, thin pieces

Steam—to put food over a pan of boiling water so the steam can cook it

Stir—to continuously mix food with a spoon

Stir-fry—to cook food on the stovetop in a very hot pan while stirring constantly

Toast—to brown the surface of a food by heating

Whip—to beat rapidly with a whisk or electric mixer

Yummy!

Each of the clues suggests a word. Write the word on the dotted lines, then fill each letter into the grid. Work back and forth between the clues and the grid until you get the silly answer to the riddle.

A. **Lettuce tossed with dressing**

....
1   25   17   18   22

B. **Melted rock from a volcano**

....
26   16   12   14

C. **Sound that bounces back**

....
13   5   10   2

D. **Back edge of the foot**

....
3   24   21   8

E. **An adult boy**

....
23   11   19

F. **A baby bear**

....
20   7   15

G. **A female deer**

....
9   6   4

Why did the circus lion eat the tightrope walker?

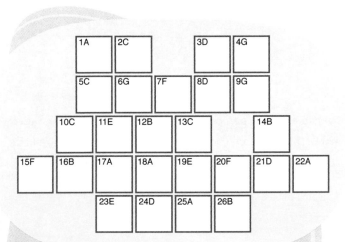

| 1A | 2C | | 3D | 4G |
| 5C | 6G | 7F | 8D | 9G |

| 10C | 11E | 12B | 13C | | 14B |

| 15F | 16B | 17A | 18A | 19E | 20F | 21D | 22A |

| 23E | 24D | 25A | 26B |

Measuring Ingredients

To make a recipe properly, it is necessary to measure ingredients accurately. Your cooking tools should include measuring spoons and a set of measuring cups for both liquid and dry ingredients.

Glass or clear plastic measuring cups are used to measure liquids like milk and water. These cups are marked with different measurements (¼ cup, ⅓ cup, ½ cup, ⅔ cup, ¾ cup, and 1 cup) so you can see how high to fill them.

Stacked measuring cups for dry ingredients come in specific sizes. The sets are usually made from either plastic or metal, and there are separate cups for each measurement. You usually use these cups for dry ingredients, like flour and sugar.

Measuring spoons measure small amounts of either liquid or dry ingredients.

Make sure to fill the cup or spoon evenly to the top. Level off dry ingredients using a blunt knife or spatula. Soft ingredients, like brown sugar, peanut butter, or shortening, get packed in, as shown in the illustration on this page.

Measuring Brown Sugar

Measuring Soft Ingredients

Measuring Liquids

Measuring Dry Ingredients

Measuring Butter

Using Measuring Spoon

Common Cooking Abbreviations and Equivalent Measures

Most recipes use abbreviations for the measurements of your ingredients. Here is a quick guide to let you know what standard abbreviations mean:

COMMON ABBREVIATIONS		
ABBREVIATION	=	MEASUREMENT
t. or tsp.	=	teaspoon
T. or Tbsp.	=	tablespoon
c.	=	cup
pt.	=	pint
qt.	=	quart
oz.	=	ounce
lb.	=	pound
pkg.	=	package

Measuring Spoon Math

Margarita is baking a cake. The recipe calls for 2 cups flour, 1 ½ cups sugar, and ¼ cup cocoa powder. Margarita only has a tablespoon with which to measure. How many tablespoons (Tbsp.) will she need of each ingredient?

FLOUR = _____ TBSP.

SUGAR = _____ TBSP.

COCOA = _____ TBSP.

Hint: 1 cup = 16 Tbsp.

It is also helpful to know what different measurements equal. This quick reference will give you the basics:

EQUIVALENT MEASURES		
RECIPE MEASUREMENT	=	WHAT IT EQUALS (EQUIVALENT)
a pinch/dash	=	less than ⅛ teaspoon
3 teaspoons	=	1 tablespoon
¼ cup	=	4 tablespoons
⅓ cup	=	5 tablespoons + 1 teaspoon
½ cup	=	8 tablespoons
⅔ cup	=	10 tablespoons + 2 teaspoons
½ pint	=	1 cup
1 cup (dry ingredients)	=	16 tablespoons
1 cup (liquid)	=	8 ounces
2 cups (liquid)	=	1 pint or ½ quart
4 cups (liquid)	=	1 quart
4 quarts (liquid)	=	1 gallon
8 ounces	=	½ pound
16 ounces (liquid)	=	1 pint or ½ quart
16 ounces	=	1 pound
32 ounces (liquid)	=	1 quart
64 ounces (liquid)	=	½ gallon
1 liter (liquid)	=	1.06 quarts
1 quart (liquid)	=	0.95 liter

What You Need to Know about Nutrition

Have you ever wondered why we eat? We eat to keep nourished, to stay alive. Just like a car needs gasoline, people need fuel, and food is the fuel that keeps us moving. Without it, we could not survive.

Nutrients

Every food we eat has substances in it called nutrients. When we talk about nutrition, we are talking about these nutrients, all the substances that are in our food. There are more than fifty different nutrients—some you have probably heard of, like protein, fat, carbohydrates, vitamins, minerals, and even water. All these nutrients work together in our bodies to help us grow, give us energy, and help us stay healthy.

MyPlate

To help people understand the importance of good nutrition, the United States Department of Agriculture, or USDA, has created a learning program called MyPlate, which can help you learn how to balance the foods you eat. This colorful plate is divided into four sections—vegetables, fruits, grains, and good protein foods. A fifth group, dairy, is also included. When you fill the sections of the plate properly, it helps you to eat balanced, nutritious meals.

Of course, you might not eat all the foods at every meal of the day, but do your best to get as many in as possible. And, if you skip one type of food at one meal, make sure to include it at the next. You can even make a game out of it.

Here are the food groups shown on MyPlate.

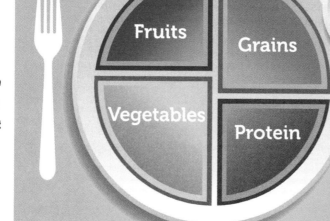

The USDA program MyPlate shows you what you should eat to stay healthy.

Eating the right combination of foods will help your body to be healthy now and in the future. It's up to you to make good choices. Here are some tips:

- **Eat more fruits and vegetables. Fill half of your plate with these.**

- **Try to pick whole grains, like brown rice, oatmeal, and whole-wheat bread.**

- **Drink milk instead of sugary drinks. Occasionally, chocolate milk is fine too!**

- **Add protein to as many meals as you can. Chicken, fish, eggs, and beef are all good options.**

- **Make sweets a treat, but not all the time. They shouldn't replace the better foods.**

- **Try to get about 1 hour of exercise or activity in every day. Ride, dance, run, play—it's all good and all fun too!**

GREEN	*Vegetables*	Vegetables supply your body with vitamins and minerals. The darker green and orange ones give you even more.
RED	*Fruits*	Fruits of all colors, sizes, and shapes provide helpful nutrients to keep your body healthy.
ORANGE	*Grains*	You'll get lots of fiber in these foods—especially the whole grains. Try to make half the grains you choose whole grains.
PURPLE	*Proteins*	These are important to build and strengthen the muscles and tissues in your body. They also have lots of vitamins and minerals.
BLUE	*Dairy*	Milk is good for your bones. It provides your body with lots of calcium. Cheese and yogurt are part of this group too.

How to Read a Nutrition Label

Nutrition Facts

8 servings per container

Serving size   2/3 cup (55g)

Amount per serving

Calories   230

	% Daily Value*
Total Fat 8g	**10%**
Saturated Fat 1g	**5%**
Trans Fat 0g	
Cholesterol 0mg	**0%**
Sodium 160mg	**7%**
Total Carbohydrate 37g	**13%**
Dietary Fiber 4g	**14%**
Total Sugars 12g	
Includes 10g Added Sugars	**20%**
Protein 3g	
Vitamin D 2mcg	10%
Calcium 260mg	20%
Iron 8mg	45%
Potassium 240mg	6%

* The % Daily Value (DV) tells you how much a nutrient in a serving of food contributes to a daily diet. 2,000 calories a day is used for general nutrition advice.

Look on food packages for the part marked "Nutrition Facts." This section provides you with information on how much nutrition this particular food provides, as well as information about how many servings are in the package, how big a serving is, and how many calories there are in a serving.

Looking at the Nutrition Facts food label, can you answer the following questions?

- *How many calories does this food have?*

- *How much sugar is in this food?*

The nutrients listed here are measured in what we call grams and milligrams. They're very tiny amounts, but they are very important to your body. Some vitamins and minerals are also listed by percentages, telling you how much the food gives you based on what you need each day. Now find a Nutrition Facts label on a food package at home. Can you determine what's in the foods you eat?

A Tasty Puzzle

You can't eat this puzzle, but you can use your "noodle" to cook up some answers. We left you a T-A-S-T-Y hint!

ACROSS

2 This form of fat might be listed on food packages as "vegetable _____."

4 These are the parts of food that your body uses to grow, have energy, and stay healthy. Junk food has very few of them.

8 To learn about the ingredients in your food, read the _____!

DOWN

1 You need six to eight glasses of this nutrient every day.

3 Bees make this form of sugar.

5 It's OK to have "junk food" once in a while, as a special _____.

6 Squirrels like this food, which contains a lot of protein and fat.

7 Eat fruits when you crave a sweet treat instead of foods high in _____.

Chapter 2

WAKE UP TO A GOOD BREAKFAST

Have you ever heard that breakfast is the most important meal of the day? Well, it's true! Breakfast gives you a boost of energy for the day—enough energy to work, play, think, read, and concentrate.

Even if you're not very hungry in the morning, eating something will energize and refuel your body. Even a small breakfast is better than no breakfast.

AVOCADO TOAST

Mashed avocado piled on toast makes a delicious and healthy breakfast. Try topping the toast with Fried Eggs (see recipe later in this chapter) for an even heartier meal.

SERVES 2

1 medium avocado

1 teaspoon lemon juice

2 thick slices sourdough or whole-wheat bread

1 teaspoon olive oil

¼ teaspoon salt

¼ teaspoon ground black pepper

½ teaspoon dried parsley

1 tablespoon roasted sunflower seeds

1. With an adult's help, cut the avocado in half and remove and discard the pit. Scoop the avocado into a medium bowl.

2. Use a potato masher to mash the avocado until it's almost smooth. Add the lemon juice to the avocado and stir together using a wooden spoon.

3. Toast the bread in a toaster oven or toaster. Place the toasted bread on two small plates.

4. Drizzle the oil over the slices of toast, then spread half of the avocado mixture on each slice.

5. Sprinkle with the salt, pepper, parsley, and sunflower seeds. Serve right away.

PER SERVING

Calories: 300 | Fat: 20g | Sodium: 490mg | Carbohydrates: 28g | Fiber: 7g | Sugar: 1g | Protein: 6g

How to Tell If an Avocado Is Ripe

There are a few ways to find out if an avocado is ripe and ready to eat:

1. Ripe avocados are darker green in color, almost beginning to turn black.

2. The stem at the top easily pops off.

3. The avocado feels lightly soft, but not mushy, when you squeeze it.

BREAKFAST FRUITY POPS

Fruit pops are fun to make for breakfast. You can make different kinds of pops—try using apple or pear slices, pineapple chunks, or whole blackberries. If you don't eat these right away, wrap them in plastic wrap and save them for another day.

SERVES 2

2 graham crackers

1 (6-ounce) container low-fat vanilla yogurt

1 medium banana, peeled

4 large strawberries, stems removed

6 popsicle sticks

1. Cut a piece of parchment paper to fit inside a 9-inch square baking pan and place it inside the pan.

2. Put the graham crackers in a plastic zip-top bag. Seal the bag and place it on a flat surface. Using a rolling pin, crush the graham crackers into fine crumbs. Pour the crumbs onto a shallow plate.

3. Spoon the yogurt into a small bowl.

4. Cut the banana in half. Poke a popsicle stick into the middle of the cut part of each banana half. Poke a popsicle stick into the stem end of each strawberry.

5. Dip the fruit pops into the yogurt and turn them around until they're coated.

6. Roll the yogurt-covered fruit in the graham cracker crumbs until they're covered. Place the pops in the baking pan.

7. Put the pan in the freezer for 30 minutes. Remove from the freezer and serve.

PER SERVING

Calories: 150 | Fat: 2g | Sodium: 70mg | Carbohydrates: 31g | Fiber: 2g | Sugar: 22g | Protein: 5g

Bunches of Bagels

Figure out the topping on these bagels by reading the letters in a circle. The trick is to know which letter comes first, and whether to read to the right or to the left. Then decide which bagel and topping combo you would want to eat for breakfast!

#1

CINNAMON-RAISIN FRENCH TOAST

Try topping your toast with your favorite syrup, or sprinkle it with powdered sugar. For even more sweet cinnamon flavor in your French toast, add 1 tablespoon of sugar and ½ teaspoon of cinnamon to the egg mixture.

SERVES 4

2 large eggs

⅓ cup milk

2 tablespoons butter, divided

8 slices cinnamon-raisin bread

1. In a wide bowl, beat the eggs and milk with a whisk.
2. Melt 1 tablespoon of the butter in a large skillet over medium heat.
3. One by one, dip four slices of bread in the egg mixture, coating both sides, then place them in the hot skillet. Cook 1–2 minutes on each side until golden brown. Use a spatula to move the French toast to a plate.
4. Add the rest of the butter to the skillet, dip the remaining four slices of bread in the egg mixture, and cook 1–2 minutes on each side until golden brown. Use the spatula to move the French toast to the plate. Serve warm.

PER SERVING

Calories: 300 | Fat: 12g | Sodium: 300mg | Carbohydrates: 37g | Fiber: 0g | Sugar: 17g | Protein: 10g

divided:
....
When this word follows an item in the ingredients list of a recipe, it means that the listed amount of the ingredient is not used all at once; the ingredient will be needed in more than one step of the recipe.

APPLE-CINNAMON OATMEAL

DIFFICULTY:
MEDIUM

You can also add raisins or nuts to this oatmeal if you like.

SERVES 4

1 cup rolled oats (not instant)

1 cup milk

1 cup water

1 tablespoon light brown sugar

1 large apple, peeled, cored, and finely chopped

1 teaspoon ground cinnamon

1. Combine the oats, milk, water, brown sugar, and apple in a large saucepan.
2. Heat the mixture over medium-high heat until it begins to boil, stirring occasionally with a wooden spoon.
3. Reduce the heat to low and let the mixture simmer for about 2–3 minutes, continuing to stir.
4. When the oatmeal gets thick and mushy, remove it from the heat. Pour the oatmeal into bowls and sprinkle it with the cinnamon before serving.

PER SERVING

Calories: 160 | Fat: 3.5g | Sodium: 25mg | Carbohydrates: 29g | Fiber: 4g | Sugar: 13g | Protein: 5g

Bunches of Bagels

Figure out the topping on these bagels by reading the letters in a circle. The trick is to know which letter comes first, and whether to read to the right or to the left. Then decide which bagel and topping combo you would want to eat for breakfast!

#2

CINNAMON-SUGAR DOUGHNUT BALLS

DIFFICULTY: MEDIUM

Make a batch of these fun little doughnuts and take them along in the car or on the bus to eat on your way to school. Try adding some mini chocolate chips to the dough when you roll the balls, if you like.

SERVES 10

½ teaspoon ground cinnamon

2 tablespoons sugar

1 (6-ounce) can refrigerated biscuit dough (5 biscuits)

2 tablespoons butter

1. Preheat the oven to 350°F.
2. Put the cinnamon and sugar in a large zip-top plastic bag. Shake the bag until the mixture is combined. Set it aside.
3. Unroll the biscuit dough on a cutting board and separate the biscuits. Use a knife to cut each biscuit into four pieces. (You can also use your hands to break them into pieces.) Roll each piece of dough into a ball and place the balls on a large baking sheet. Bake 10–12 minutes until light brown in color. Remove the baking sheet from the oven using pot holders. Place the baking sheet on a cooling rack and let the balls cool for 1 minute.
4. Cut the butter into four pieces and place the pieces in a medium microwave-safe bowl. Microwave the butter on high for 20–30 seconds or until the butter is melted.
5. Put five or six balls in the bowl with the butter and roll them around until they are well coated. Drop the coated balls into the bag of cinnamon sugar and shake the bag until the balls are covered with cinnamon sugar. Remove them from the bag and place them on a plate.
6. Repeat with the rest of the balls, butter, and cinnamon sugar. Serve right away.

PER SERVING

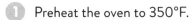

Calories: 70 | Fat: 3.5g | Sodium: 140mg | Carbohydrates: 10g | Fiber: 0g | Sugar: 3g | Protein: 1g

HOMEMADE GRANOLA

Eat granola as a snack or sprinkled on your favorite flavor of yogurt, or try it with milk for a quick, healthy breakfast cereal.

MAKES 3 CUPS

1½ cups rolled oats (not instant)

½ cup sunflower seeds

½ cup raisins or dried cranberries

¼ cup chopped walnuts

2 tablespoons melted butter

1 tablespoon vegetable oil

1 tablespoon molasses

2 tablespoons light corn syrup

1. Preheat the oven to 375°F.
2. In a large bowl, combine the oats, sunflower seeds, raisins or cranberries, and walnuts.
3. In a small bowl, stir together the melted butter, oil, molasses, and corn syrup.

4. Pour the butter mixture over the oat mixture and stir it well with a wooden spoon.
5. Spread the granola into a 9-by-13-inch baking pan. Bake 10 minutes. While the granola is cooking, stir the mixture once or twice to help it dry out and keep it from burning.

6. Use pot holders to remove the pan from the oven and stir the granola again. Let it cool before serving. Store leftover granola in an airtight container.

PER SERVING (½ CUP)

Calories: 290 | Fat: 16g | Sodium: 80mg |
Carbohydrates: 35g | Fiber: 3g | Sugar: 13g |
Protein: 6g

molasses:
....

The thick brown syrup that is separated
from raw sugar during the refining process.

FRIED EGGS

Make Fried Eggs the way you like them—sunny-side up (cooked only on one side so you can see the yellow yolk) or over easy (cooked on both sides).

SERVES 1

2 large eggs

1 tablespoon butter

⅛ teaspoon salt

⅛ teaspoon ground black pepper

1. Crack the eggs into a small bowl. Try to do this gently so you don't break the yolks.
2. Melt the butter in a medium skillet over medium heat.
3. Pour the eggs into the skillet and cook them until the whites are set (turn white), about 2 minutes.

4. If you like your eggs sunny-side up, do not flip the eggs over. Cook them until the eggs are set and not runny. If you like your eggs over easy, gently flip them over with a spatula (still trying to not break the yolks) and cook another minute.

5. Using the spatula, move the eggs to a plate, sprinkle with the salt and pepper, and eat right away.

PER SERVING

Calories: 250 | Fat: 21g | Sodium: 440mg |
Carbohydrates: 1g | Fiber: 0g | Sugar: 0g |
Protein: 13g

How to Crack an Egg

There are a couple of ways to open a raw egg into a bowl. You can crack the egg gently on the edge of the bowl, then pull apart the two halves of the shell so the egg drops into the bowl. Or, holding the egg over the bowl in one hand, use a butter knife to crack open the shell.

CHEESY SCRAMBLED EGGS

Try combining several cheeses to create your own favorite cheesy eggs.

SERVES 2

4 large eggs

¼ cup milk

½ teaspoon salt

⅛ teaspoon ground black pepper

¼ cup shredded Cheddar cheese

1 tablespoon butter

1. Crack the eggs into a small bowl.
2. Use a whisk to beat the eggs until they are light yellow and mixed well. Add the milk, salt, pepper, and cheese to the eggs and whisk again.
3. Melt the butter in a medium skillet over medium heat.
4. Pour the egg mixture into the heated skillet. Use a spatula to move the eggs around as they cook.
5. When the eggs are cooked and no longer runny (about 3 minutes), remove them from the skillet and serve.

PER SERVING

Calories: 270 | Fat: 21g | Sodium: 840mg | Carbohydrates: 3g | Fiber: 0g | Sugar: 2g | Protein: 17g

Egg-ceptional Facts

- Eggs from many animals are edible, including eggs from ducks, geese, pigeons, turtles, ostriches, and even crocodiles.

- In 1493, Christopher Columbus took chickens on his second voyage to the New World so the sailors would have eggs to eat during their travels.

- To tell whether an egg is raw or has been cooked, spin it on its pointed end. If it spins, it is cooked; if it falls over, it is raw.

- Since early times, people have decorated eggs to give as gifts at Easter and other times of the year.

- The world's most famous eggs were decorated by Russian jeweler Carl Fabergé. He made beautiful eggs for the Russian royal family for Easter and other special occasions. They were made with gems and precious metals like gold and silver, and today they are worth millions of dollars.

HARD-BOILED EGGS

Hard-Boiled Eggs are so easy to make. Keep some in the refrigerator for an anytime snack.

DIFFICULTY:
EASY

SERVES 2

2 large eggs

1. Place the eggs in a small saucepan. Fill the pan with enough water to cover the eggs. Put the saucepan over high heat and bring the water to a boil. Reduce the heat to low, cover the pan, and let the water simmer for 12 minutes.

2. Remove the saucepan from the heat. With a slotted spoon, move the eggs to a medium bowl. Add cold water to the bowl. Keep the eggs in the water for 10 minutes.

3. Remove the eggs from the water. Gently crack the eggshells and peel them off. Serve right away or keep them in a covered container in the refrigerator.

PER SERVING

Calories: 70 | Fat: 5g | Sodium: 70mg |
Carbohydrates: 0g | Fiber: 0g | Sugar: 0g | Protein: 6g

Bunches of Bagels

Figure out the topping on these bagels by reading the letters in a circle. The trick is to know which letter comes first, and whether to read to the right or to the left. Then decide which bagel and topping combo you would want to eat for breakfast!

#3

DIFFICULTY: MEDIUM

BLUEBERRY MUFFINS

These berry-filled muffins are great for breakfast or for a snack after school.

MAKES 12 MUFFINS

1½ cups fresh blueberries

1½ cups all-purpose flour

⅔ cup sugar

½ teaspoon baking soda

½ teaspoon salt

2 large eggs

⅓ cup vegetable oil

½ cup milk

1. Preheat the oven to 375°F. Spray a 12-cup muffin tin with nonstick cooking spray or line the muffin tin with paper liners.

2. Put the blueberries in a colander and rinse them off. Set the colander aside to drain.

3. In a large bowl, combine the flour, sugar, baking soda, and salt.

4. In a small bowl, combine the eggs, oil, and milk.

5. Add the egg mixture to the flour mixture and stir together with a wooden spoon until they are just blended. Do not overmix. Very gently stir the blueberries into the batter.

6. Pour the batter into the prepared muffin tin so each cup is about two-thirds full.

7. Bake 18–20 minutes or until the muffins are lightly browned and cooked throughout. Using pot holders, remove the muffin tin from the oven and place it on a cooling rack. Cool 5 minutes in the muffin tin, then carefully turn the tin over to remove the muffins.

8. Serve warm or let the muffins cool before eating.

PER SERVING (1 MUFFIN)

Calories: 170 | Fat: 7g | Sodium: 170mg | Carbohydrates: 25g | Fiber: 1g | Sugar: 13g | Protein: 3g

Test to Be Sure

To test for doneness, insert a toothpick into the center of a muffin. If the toothpick comes out clean, the muffins are done. If there is batter on the toothpick, the muffins need to cook another 1–2 minutes. Then test again with a clean toothpick.

CHOCOLATE CHIP PANCAKES

DIFFICULTY: **MEDIUM**

Try these as a special treat after a sleepover. They are simple to make, and so much fun to eat! Serve the pancakes with your favorite syrup or sprinkled with powdered sugar.

SERVES 4

1 cup all-purpose flour

1 tablespoon sugar

1 teaspoon baking powder

½ cup semisweet chocolate chips

1 cup milk

1 large egg, lightly beaten

2 tablespoons vegetable oil, divided

1. Combine the flour, sugar, baking powder, and chocolate chips in a large bowl.
2. In a small bowl, combine the milk and the egg.
3. Pour the milk mixture into the flour mixture and mix together with a whisk until smooth.
4. Pour 1 tablespoon of the oil into a large skillet and heat it over medium heat. Drop about 2 tablespoonfuls of pancake batter onto the hot skillet for each pancake. You should be able to fit three or four pancakes in the pan.
5. Cook until the edges become brown and the batter becomes bubbly, about 2–3 minutes.
6. Flip the pancakes over with a spatula and cook until the other side is browned too, about 1 minute. Continue cooking the rest of the pancakes until all the batter is used up. (Add the rest of the oil to the pan as you need to.) Serve right away.

PER SERVING

Calories: 370 | Fat: 18g | Sodium: 180mg | Carbohydrates: 49g | Fiber: 1g | Sugar: 23g | Protein: 8g

Food Trivia

The world's biggest pancake weighed in at 49 feet in diameter and weighed 6,614 pounds. Two construction cranes were needed to flip it!

MINI BITE-SIZED BLUEBERRY PANCAKES

Watch these pancakes puff up as they cook. Make them as a weekend treat, but be sure to save the extras to reheat for breakfast during the week.

SERVES 6

1½ cups all-purpose flour

1 tablespoon sugar

1½ teaspoons baking powder

½ teaspoon baking soda

½ teaspoon salt

1 large egg, lightly beaten

1 tablespoon melted butter

1½ cups low-fat buttermilk

½ cup fresh blueberries

3 teaspoons vegetable oil, divided

1. In a large bowl, combine the flour, sugar, baking powder, baking soda, and salt.
2. Add the egg, butter, and buttermilk. Mix together with a whisk until smooth. Carefully stir in the blueberries with a wooden spoon.
3. In a large skillet, heat 1 teaspoon of the oil over medium heat. Using a 1 tablespoon measuring spoon, drop pancake batter onto the hot skillet. You will have room for about six to eight pancakes at a time.
4. Cook until the edges become brown and the batter becomes bubbly, about 1–2 minutes.
5. Flip the pancakes over with a spatula and cook until the other side is browned too, about 1 minute. Continue cooking the rest of the pancakes until all the batter is used up. (Add the rest of the oil to the pan as you need to.)

PER SERVING

Calories: 190 | Fat: 6g | Sodium: 570mg | Carbohydrates: 29g | Fiber: 1g | Sugar: 7g | Protein: 6g

Star Berries

Native Americans called blueberries "star berries," because the blossom end usually has five points, like a star. Look at the end of a blueberry. Can you see the star?

Make Your Own

If you don't have buttermilk, you can use this instead: Measure 1½ tablespoons of lemon juice or white vinegar into a 2-cup glass measuring cup. Then add milk to make 1½ cups total. Set the measuring cup aside for 5 minutes. You'll be able to see that the lemon juice or vinegar thickens the milk.

EGG AND CHEESE BREAKFAST BURRITO

Burritos are favorites for lunch and dinner; why not try one for breakfast?

SERVES 1

1 large egg

1 teaspoon vegetable oil

1 (6-inch) flour tortilla

1 tablespoon shredded Cheddar cheese

1½ teaspoons salsa

1. Crack the egg into a small bowl and stir it with a whisk.
2. Heat the oil in a small skillet over medium heat. Add the egg and cook, stirring with a spatula, for 2–3 minutes until set.
3. Place the scrambled egg in the center of the tortilla. Top with the cheese and salsa. Roll up and eat.

PER SERVING

Calories: 240 | Fat: 14g | Sodium: 470mg | Carbohydrates: 17g | Fiber: 0g | Sugar: 1g | Protein: 11g

Bunches of Bagels

Figure out the topping on these bagels by reading the letters in a circle. The trick is to know which letter comes first, and whether to read to the right or to the left. Then decide which bagel and topping combo you would want to eat for breakfast!

What Does *Burrito* Mean?

In Spanish, *burrito* means "little donkey" because a stuffed burrito can contain a lot of different things just like a donkey can carry a lot of different things.

BLUEBERRY AND QUINOA BREAKFAST BOWL

DIFFICULTY:
MEDIUM

If you like oatmeal, try a quinoa bowl. Quinoa is sometimes called a "superfood" because it has so many health benefits. It's high in protein, vitamins, and fiber.

SERVES 2

½ cup uncooked white or red quinoa

1 cup unsweetened almond milk

1 tablespoon light brown sugar

½ cup blueberries

¼ cup slivered almonds

1. Put the quinoa in a fine-mesh strainer or colander (make sure the holes are very small) and rinse it under cold water. After all the water drains out, put the quinoa in a medium saucepan.

2. Stir in the almond milk and brown sugar.

3. Heat the saucepan over medium-high heat until the mixture starts to boil, then reduce the heat to medium-low. Stir the mixture with a wooden spoon, then simmer it for 12–15 minutes until the quinoa is soft and the milk is absorbed into the quinoa.

4. Remove the pan from the heat and stir the quinoa again. Cover the pan and set it aside for 5 minutes.

5. Uncover the pan and spoon the quinoa into two bowls. Top each bowl with half of the blueberries and almonds. Serve right away.

PER SERVING

Calories: 310 | Fat: 10g | Sodium: 90mg | Carbohydrates: 49g | Fiber: 6g | Sugar: 14g | Protein: 10g

quinoa:

The seed of a South American flowering plant. It is called a superfood because it's high in protein and other nutrients. There are more than 120 varieties of quinoa.

Make It Your Own

You can make this dish in lots of different ways. Try another kind of berry or
canned fruit. Replace the granola with
your favorite cereal, crushed. Use a
different kind of fruit jam or preserves
to drizzle on top. Or replace the jam
with maple syrup or honey.

BREAKFAST BANANA SPLIT

If you love banana splits, why not make one for breakfast? Find a special ice cream dish to serve it in, and you'll feel like you've got a real treat!

SERVES 1

1 medium banana, peeled

1 cup low-fat cottage cheese

¼ cup sliced strawberries

¼ cup canned mandarin oranges in syrup, drained

2 tablespoons strawberry jam

¼ cup granola

1. Cut the banana in half lengthwise. Place both halves side by side in a bowl or ice cream dish.
2. Use a small ice cream scoop to scoop the cottage cheese on top of the banana. Top with the strawberries and mandarin oranges.
3. Put the jam in a small microwave-safe bowl and microwave on high for 5–10 seconds until it melts and becomes pourable. Remove the bowl from the microwave and drizzle the melted jam over the banana split. Sprinkle with the granola.
4. Eat immediately.

PER SERVING

Calories: 540 | Fat: 7g | Sodium: 700mg |
Carbohydrates: 95g | Fiber: 4g | Sugar: 63g | Protein: 29g

Banana Trivia

A bunch of bananas is called a "hand" and sometimes has as many as ten to fifteen bananas on it. Each banana is called a "finger."

Bunches of Bagels

Figure out the topping on these bagels by reading the letters in a circle. The trick is to know which letter comes first, and whether to read to the right or to the left. Then decide which bagel and topping combo you would want to eat for breakfast!

#5

Breakfast Scrambles

First, unscramble all the words in the frying pan. Then use them to complete the riddles.

SHOGT SGEG
ASTOT OACEBN
NBCOA EGLS

HINT: These breakfast orders are silly—not normal. Think twice before you write your answers!

What does a dog have for breakfast?

Woofles!

What does a centipede have for breakfast?
_____ AND _____

What does a lighthouse keeper have for breakfast?
_____ AND _____

What does a spook have for breakfast?
_____ _____

What's So Funny

Two cooks are telling each other a joke, but they are speaking in "Cooktalk." Can you figure out their secret language so you can join in the fun?

WEGGHEGGAEGGTEGG   TEGGWEGGOEGG
TEGGHEGGIEGGNEGGGEGGSEGG
CEGGAEGGNEGG'TEGG   YEGGOEGGUEGG
HEGGAEGGVEGGE   FEGGOEGGREGG
BEGGREGGEEGGAEGGKEGGFEGGAEGGSEGGTEGG?

LEGGUEGGNEGGCEGGHEGG   AEGGNEGGDEGG
DEGGIEGGNEGGNEGGEEGGREGG!!

Chapter 3

LUNCHES, SANDWICHES, AND BROWN BAG IDEAS

Lunchtime is fun time. Whether you are making a weekend lunch at home or packing a lunch for school, find foods that you like best. Try new things and experiment with old favorites. You'll soon find that the more you help in the kitchen, the better you will learn to like the foods you make!

GRILLED CHEESE AND TOMATO SANDWICH

What's better than a warm and crispy grilled cheese sandwich? This sandwich goes great with Tasty Tomato Soup (see recipe later in this chapter).

SERVES 1

2 slices whole-wheat bread

2 slices American or Cheddar cheese

2 thin slices tomato

1 teaspoon butter

1. Make a sandwich with the cheese and tomato between the two slices of bread.
2. Melt the butter in a small skillet over medium heat.
3. Place the sandwich in the skillet and cook it for about 2 minutes on each side, until the cheese is melted and the bread becomes slightly browned and crispy. Use a spatula to move the sandwich to a plate.

PER SERVING

Calories: 300 | Fat: 15g | Sodium: 860mg | Carbohydrates: 27g | Fiber: 0g | Sugar: 0g | Protein: 13g

Toast or Not?

Here's a cooking experiment. Lay two slices of bread side by side. Spread one with butter and leave the other plain. Toast both slices in a toaster oven and see what happens. The plain one will toast, but the one with butter will not. Why? Because the fat from the butter keeps the bread moist and soft and prevents it from drying out.

Fun Fact

Did you know that cheese is not really a favorite food for mice? They prefer sweeter foods and grains. Sure, they'll eat cheese if it's the only thing around, as most animals would, but they don't particularly love it.

CHEESIEST MACARONI AND CHEESE

Homemade mac and cheese is delicious, gooey with melted cheese, and way better than the stuff that comes in a box. It takes a little more time, but it's worth it!

SERVES 4

1 cup uncooked elbow macaroni

2 tablespoons butter

2 tablespoons all-purpose flour

¼ teaspoon salt

¼ teaspoon ground black pepper

¼ teaspoon dry mustard

¼ teaspoon Worcestershire sauce

1 cup milk

1½ cups shredded Cheddar cheese

2 tablespoons seasoned bread crumbs

1. Preheat the oven to 350°F. Spray a 2-quart casserole dish with nonstick cooking spray.

2. Pour water into a large saucepan until it is two-thirds full. Place the saucepan over high heat and bring it to a boil. Add the macaroni and cook for 9 minutes, stirring occasionally. Place a colander in the sink and ask an adult to help you carefully pour the macaroni and water into the colander to drain.

3. Melt the butter in the same saucepan over medium heat. When it's melted, reduce the heat to low.

4. Stirring the whole time, add the flour, salt, pepper, mustard, and Worcestershire sauce. When the mixture is smooth, add the milk and cheese. Continue stirring until the cheese melts and the sauce is creamy and smooth. This should take about 4–5 minutes.

5. Stir the macaroni into the cheese sauce.

Play It Safe

Always use pot holders or oven mitts to touch hot pans and dishes. You may not realize how hot something is until you've picked it up, so it's always better to start out with your hands protected.

6 Pour the mixture into the casserole dish. Sprinkle the bread crumbs over the top.

7 Bake 30–40 minutes, or until the casserole is lightly browned on top. Using pot holders, remove the casserole dish from the oven. Let the macaroni and cheese sit about 5–10 minutes before serving so the cheesy, creamy sauce has a chance to thicken.

Fun Fact

Pasta is one of the most popular foods for kids. Statistics show that kids eat 62 pounds of pasta each year—more than any other age group.

PER SERVING

Calories: 340 | Fat: 17g | Sodium: 570mg | Carbohydrates: 31g | Fiber: 0g | Sugar: 4g | Protein: 17g

Silly Slice

The letters in each column go in the squares directly below them, but not in the same order. Blue squares show the spaces between words. When you have correctly filled in the grid, you will have the silly answer to the riddle.

What's the difference between a person who is not smart and a pizza?

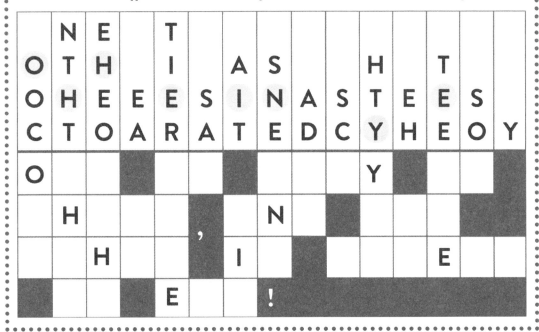

TASTY TUNA MELTS

Tuna melts are delicious for lunch or as an afternoon snack. For a fun change, bake a potato in the microwave, top it with tuna and cheese, and bake it. You will have a Tuna Melt Potato!

SERVES 4

2 English muffins or bagels, split in half

1 (5-ounce) can chunk light tuna in water

1½ tablespoons mayonnaise

¼ cup shredded Cheddar cheese

1. Preheat the oven to 350°F.
2. Place the English muffin or bagel halves on a baking sheet.
3. Use a can opener to open the tuna can (be careful of sharp edges!), then dump the tuna into a colander. Press down lightly on the tuna to remove most of the water.
4. Put the tuna in a medium bowl and use a wooden spoon or a fork to break it up into small pieces.
5. Add the mayonnaise to the tuna and mix well.
6. Top each English muffin or bagel half with the tuna mixture, then with the cheese.
7. Bake for 5–8 minutes until the cheese is melted. Use pot holders to remove the baking sheet from the oven. Serve warm.

PER SERVING

Calories: 150 | Fat: 6g | Sodium: 300mg | Carbohydrates: 13g | Fiber: 0g | Sugar: 1g | Protein: 11g

EGGY SALAD

DIFFICULTY:
EASY

Egg salad can be used as a sandwich spread or as a dip with crackers or Parmesan Pita Chips (Chapter 4). Either way, it tastes so good, you'll be surprised how easy it is to make.

SERVES 2

2 Hard-Boiled Eggs (Chapter 2)

1 tablespoon mayonnaise

½ teaspoon celery salt

¼ teaspoon ground black pepper

¼ teaspoon paprika

1. Peel the shells from the Hard-Boiled Eggs.
2. Place the eggs in a medium bowl and mash them with a potato masher or a fork.
3. Add the mayonnaise, celery salt, and pepper. Mix well.
4. Sprinkle the paprika over the top of the egg salad. Serve right away or cover the bowl and refrigerate for up to two days.

PER SERVING

Calories: 120 | Fat: 10g | Sodium: 400mg | Carbohydrates: 1g | Fiber: 0g | Sugar: 0g | Protein: 6g

FLATBREAD PIZZAS

DIFFICULTY: **MEDIUM**

There are many things you can add to these flatbreads before baking. Try chopped vegetables like mushrooms, bell peppers, or broccoli. Mix it up with berries, pineapple chunks, or sliced apples and pears. Or add some meat, like pepperoni or leftover chicken. Keep trying until you find your favorite combination—it's a tasty experiment!

SERVES 4

- 1 (14.1-ounce) package rectangular flatbreads (2 flatbreads)
- 1 tablespoon olive oil
- ¼ cup pesto sauce
- 6 ounces mozzarella cheese, cut into slices
- 20 cherry or grape tomatoes, sliced
- ½ teaspoon dried basil

1. Preheat the oven to 425°F. Line a baking sheet with parchment paper or foil.

2. Place the flatbreads on the baking sheet. Use a pastry brush to brush the oil over the flatbreads. Spoon the pesto sauce onto each flatbread and spread the sauce out with the back of a wooden spoon.

3. Top the flatbreads with the cheese and tomatoes. Sprinkle the basil on top.

4. Place the baking sheet in the oven. Bake for 10–12 minutes or until the cheese is melted and golden brown. Use pot holders to remove the baking sheet from the oven. Cool the pizzas for about 10 minutes before cutting into triangles with a pizza cutter.

PER SERVING

Calories: 380 | Fat: 19g | Sodium: 870mg | Carbohydrates: 32g | Fiber: 1g | Sugar: 3g | Protein: 29g

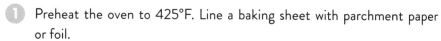

What's Your Favorite?

One of the most popular toppings for pizza in Brazil is green peas. In India, they like pickled ginger and tofu. Eel and squid are favorites in Japan. Here in the US, pepperoni is the top topping, followed by mushrooms, onions, chicken, sausage, and pineapple.

CHEESY QUESADILLAS

After trying quesadillas with just cheese, be adventurous and add some refried beans, bell peppers, Guacamole Dip (Chapter 4), black olives, or leftover cooked chicken.

SERVES 2

2 (8-inch) flour tortillas

2 tablespoons shredded Cheddar cheese

2 tablespoons sour cream

¼ cup salsa

1. Place one tortilla on a large microwave-safe plate and sprinkle it with the shredded cheese. Top with the second tortilla.

2. Cook in the microwave on high for 20–30 seconds until the cheese is melted.

3. Remove the plate from the microwave and let the quesadilla cool slightly. Use a pizza cutter or knife to cut the tortilla into six wedges.

4. Top the wedges with the sour cream and serve with the salsa for dipping.

PER SERVING

Calories: 210 | Fat: 8g | Sodium: 740mg | Carbohydrates: 28g | Fiber: 0g | Sugar: 2g | Protein: 6g

tortilla:

A round, flat, thin bread made with cornmeal or wheat flour that is commonly eaten with a topping or wrapped around a filling.

CHICKEN SALAD PUFFS

DIFFICULTY: MEDIUM

If you want to add some crunch to your puffs, try adding chopped celery or sliced almonds to the chicken salad.

SERVES 8

2 cups chopped cooked chicken breast

2 tablespoons mayonnaise

¼ cup shredded Cheddar cheese

1 (8-ounce) package crescent roll dough

1. Preheat the oven to 375°F. Spray eight cups of a 12-cup muffin tin with nonstick cooking spray.

2. Combine the chicken, mayonnaise, and cheese in a medium bowl. Mix well with a wooden spoon.

3. Open the package of crescent roll dough and unroll the dough. Separate the dough into eight pieces and press each piece into one of the eight prepared cups in the muffin tin. (It doesn't matter how you stuff them in, just be sure to cover the bottom of the cups.)

4. Evenly divide the chicken mixture and spoon some into the center of each cup.

5. Bake for 10 minutes or until the pastry is golden brown and puffy. Use pot holders to remove the muffin tin from the oven and place it on a cooling rack. Cool for 5 minutes.

6. Carefully remove the puffs from the pan and serve warm.

PER SERVING

Calories: 190 | Fat: 10g | Sodium: 430mg | Carbohydrates: 12g | Fiber: 0g | Sugar: 3g | Protein: 13g

Fun Fact

A lot of the Cheddar cheese you buy in the grocery store is orange, but that's not its natural color. Cheddar cheese is white; it only turns orange after a carrot-based food coloring has been added.

TUNA AND APPLE CRUNCH PITA SANDWICHES

A sweet crunch will make your tuna salad sandwich so much tastier. If you don't have an apple for this recipe, try a chopped pear or carrot.

SERVES 2

1 (5-ounce) can chunk light tuna in water

1 small apple

1 tablespoon mayonnaise

1 (6-inch) pita pocket bread, cut in half

1. Use a can opener to open the tuna can, then dump the tuna into a colander. Press down lightly on the tuna to remove most of the water.

2. Put the tuna in a medium bowl and use a wooden spoon or a fork to break it up into small pieces.

3. Peel, core, and chop the apple into small pieces. Add the apple pieces to the tuna in the bowl. Add the mayonnaise and mix well.

4. Stuff half of the tuna and apple mixture into each pita half. Serve right away.

PER SERVING

Calories: 230 | Fat: 6g | Sodium: 420mg | Carbohydrates: 27g | Fiber: 2g | Sugar: 8g | Protein: 17g

An Apple a Day

You've probably heard the saying "An apple a day keeps the doctor away." Apples are definitely good for you, but you should eat a variety of fruits and vegetables to stay healthy. What's more, the skins of apples and other foods are very good for you, so remember to leave them on whenever you can.

CREAMY CORN CHOWDER

DIFFICULTY:
MEDIUM

A chowder is a type of soup or stew that's usually creamy and filled with lots of vegetables, like potatoes, or seafood. Chowders are thick, creamy, and filling.

SERVES 6

1 tablespoon vegetable oil

1 small onion, peeled and finely chopped

3 medium potatoes, peeled and chopped

2 cups plus 2 tablespoons water, divided

½ teaspoon salt

¼ teaspoon ground black pepper

2 tablespoons cornstarch

2 (15.25-ounce) cans corn, drained

2 cups milk

2 tablespoons butter

1. Heat the oil in a large saucepan over medium heat.

2. Add the onion and cook for about 5 minutes, stirring frequently. Add the potatoes, 2 cups water, salt, and pepper.

3. Turn up the heat to high and cook until the mixture boils. Reduce the heat to low. Simmer for about 20 minutes, or until the potatoes are soft.

4. In a small bowl, mix the cornstarch and 2 tablespoons water with a spoon until smooth. Add the mixture to the soup, then add the corn, milk, and butter. Stir to combine.

5. Continue simmering the soup for another 20 minutes, stirring every once in a while.

6. Remove the pan from the heat and cool for 10 minutes before serving.

PER SERVING

Calories: 300 | Fat: 11g | Sodium: 530mg | Carbohydrates: 47g | Fiber: 4g | Sugar: 11g | Protein: 8g

Kernel Count

An ear of corn has an even number of rows, usually sixteen. An average ear contains about eight hundred kernels.

The Soup Pot

Familiar soups and soup ingredients are hiding in each row of this soup pot. To find them, put one letter from the list at the top into each empty box. The letter might be in the beginning, middle, or end of the word. We gave you one important ingredient to get you started. *HINT: Each letter in the list will be used only once.*

A D H I M M N N N O O O S ~~X~~ R R

A	D	E	W	A	T	E	R		I	C	O
M	O	C	A	R			O	T	I	H	I
E	M	I	N	E			T	R	O	N	E
R	O	M	A	C			I	C	K	E	N
C	H	O	N	O			D	L	E	S	O
O	C	H	O	W			E	R	P	A	R
I	N	T	R	C			R	N	C	O	R
O	C	E	L	E			Y	T	O	M	A
C	H	E	W	O			T	O	N	O	R
B	I	B	E	A			S	O	P	I	N
O	B	N	I	B			N	I	O	N	E
P	I	N	T	O			A	T	O	R	I
C	E	L	G	U			B	O	R	I	C
M	A	P	O	T			T	O	B	R	A
R	O	L	E	R			C	E	C	H	I
N	H	O	T	A			D	S	O	U	R

TASTY TOMATO SOUP

DIFFICULTY:
MEDIUM

This soup tastes great on a cold day. It's almost as easy to make it from scratch as it is to open a can, but you'll need some help from an adult to blend the hot soup.

SERVES 4

1 (28-ounce) can whole peeled tomatoes

1 tablespoon vegetable oil

1 medium onion, peeled and chopped

3 garlic cloves, peeled and chopped

1 (14.5-ounce) can vegetable broth

1 (6-ounce) can tomato paste

1 teaspoon dried basil

1. Use a can opener to open the can of tomatoes, then pour them into a large bowl. With your clean hands, break the tomatoes up into large chunks.

2. In a large saucepan, heat the oil over medium heat. Add the onion and garlic and cook, stirring, for about 3 minutes, or until the onion is tender.

3. Add the tomatoes, cover the pan, and cook for 5 minutes to soften the tomatoes. Use the can opener to open the broth and tomato paste, then add to the pan.

4. Turn up the heat to high and cook, uncovered, until the mixture boils. Reduce the heat to medium-low, cover the pan, and simmer for 15 minutes.

5. Very carefully pour some of the soup into a blender or food processor, 1 cup at a time, until the blender is no more than half full. Do not overfill the blender. If you put too much into the blender at once, the hot liquid will overflow when you turn it on. Ask an adult to help you with this step.

6. Blend the mixture until it is smooth, then pour it into a large bowl. Pour the rest of the soup into the blender and blend it until smooth. Add the blended soup to the bowl.

7. Sprinkle the soup with the basil. Serve warm.

PER SERVING

Calories: 120 | Fat: 4g | Sodium: 710mg | Carbohydrates: 20g | Fiber: 6g | Sugar: 11g | Protein: 3g

Lunch?

Start at the letter marked with the dot, and move counterclockwise (to the left). Read every other letter to find the answer to this riddle: What is a mermaid's favorite lunch?

HINT: You will travel around twice before you find the answer.

Here you are, kids!

Thanks, Mom!

Border letters (top): A L E L P E A J H D C

Border letters (right): C N I A W R D E

Border letters (bottom): T S B H U S T A T N E

Border letters (left): A Y N F U I T

Chapter 4

SNACK TIME

Most people love to eat snacks, whether they are an after-school treat, a before-dinner appetizer, or a bedtime sweet. Snacks don't have to come out of a package. It's fun to create your own and share them with your friends and family. Snacks help satisfy your hunger pangs and carry you on to the next meal. With some imagination and ingredients you probably already have at home, you can have fun and snack well too!

PEANUT BUTTER CHIP MUFFINS

For a different twist, you can substitute ¼ cup chocolate chips for ¼ cup of the peanut butter chips.

MAKES 12 MUFFINS

1 cup smooth peanut butter

1 large egg

¼ cup granulated sugar

¼ cup light brown sugar

1 cup milk

1½ cups all-purpose flour

1 tablespoon baking powder

½ cup peanut butter chips

1. Preheat the oven to 375°F. Spray a 12-cup muffin tin with nonstick cooking spray or line the cups with paper liners.

2. In a large mixing bowl, use an electric mixer to combine the peanut butter, egg, granulated sugar, brown sugar, and milk. Beat the ingredients until smooth.

3. Add the flour and baking powder. Mix until just blended. Do not overmix.

4. Stir in the peanut butter chips with a wooden spoon.

5. Pour the batter into the prepared muffin tin so each cup is about two-thirds full.

6. Bake for 18–20 minutes or until the muffins are light brown on top. Using pot holders, remove the muffin tin from the oven and place it on a cooling rack. Cool 5 minutes in the muffin tin, then carefully turn the tin over to remove the muffins.

7. Serve warm or let the muffins cool before eating.

PER SERVING (1 MUFFIN)

Calories: 250 | Fat: 13g | Sodium: 250mg |
Carbohydrates: 29g | Fiber: 1g | Sugar: 14g |
Protein: 8g

appetizer:

A food or drink that stimulates the appetite and is usually served before a meal.

PEANUT BUTTER ENERGY SNACK BALLS

DIFFICULTY:
EASY

Keep these tasty little bites in the refrigerator for whenever you need a boost of energy. This recipe is easy to change if you want to add your favorite flavors. Try replacing the dried cranberries with mini chocolate chips or adding 2 tablespoons of shredded coconut.

MAKES 30 BALLS

1½ cups rolled oats (not instant)

½ cup chunky or smooth peanut butter

¼ cup honey

½ cup dried cranberries

1. Put all of the ingredients in a large bowl and mix well with a wooden spoon.
2. Cover the bowl with plastic wrap and put it in the refrigerator for 30 minutes.

3. Remove the dough from the refrigerator. Roll the dough with your hands into 30 balls and place the balls on a baking sheet. If the mixture sticks too much to your hands, keep washing them. If your hands are a little bit wet, it will be easier to roll the dough.
4. Place the baking sheet in the refrigerator for at least 2 hours before eating the snack balls. Keep leftovers in a covered container in the refrigerator.

PER SERVING (2 BALLS)

Calories: 110 | Fat: 5g | Sodium: 40mg | Carbohydrates: 16g | Fiber: 2g | Sugar: 9g | Protein: 3g

Play It Safe

If you're allergic to peanut butter, you can make these snack balls with sunflower butter instead.

NUTTY CARAMEL CORN

A fun snack for the fall, this fan favorite is usually made around Halloween. Make a double batch if you're having a party—it will disappear quickly!

MAKES 6 CUPS

1 (3.5-ounce) bag plain microwave popcorn, popped

1 cup dry-roasted, salted peanuts

1 cup light brown sugar

½ cup (1 stick) butter

½ cup corn syrup

¼ teaspoon salt

1. Preheat the oven to 200°F. Spray a 9-by-13-inch baking pan with non-stick cooking spray.

2. In a large bowl, combine the popcorn and peanuts.

3. In a medium saucepan, combine the brown sugar, butter, corn syrup, and salt.

4. Heat over medium-high heat until the mixture is melted and smooth, stirring constantly. This should take 4–5 minutes.

5. Remove the pan from the heat and very carefully pour the caramel mixture over the popcorn and peanuts. Use a wooden spoon to mix well until the popcorn and peanuts are coated.

6. Spread out the popcorn mixture on the prepared baking pan.

7. Bake for 1 hour, stirring every 15 minutes. Using pot holders, remove the pan from the oven and place it on a cooling rack. Let the popcorn cool for at least 30 minutes before removing it from the pan.

PER SERVING (1 CUP)

Calories: 580 | Fat: 32g | Sodium: 370mg | Carbohydrates: 70g | Fiber: 0g | Sugar: 44g | Protein: 8g

Play It Safe

The caramel mixture used to coat the popcorn gets very hot, so make sure you're careful when pouring it over the popcorn. It's a good idea to have an adult help you with this recipe.

Why Does Popcorn Pop?

Each popcorn kernel contains a small drop of water stored inside. When the kernel gets heated, the water inside turns to steam. The kernel then begins to expand as pressure starts to develop inside the hard shell. As a result, the kernel splits open and the popcorn explodes, popping the popcorn and releasing the steam. (Popcorn is a special breed of corn. You can't take a regular corn kernel and make it pop.)

PARMESAN PITA CHIPS

You can serve your pita chips with a dip or hummus or store them in an airtight container for snacking anytime.

MAKES 48 PITA CHIPS

4 (6-inch) pita pocket breads

6 tablespoons vegetable oil

½ cup grated Parmesan cheese

1½ tablespoons sesame seeds

1. Preheat the oven to 425°F. Line a large baking sheet with foil or parchment paper.
2. Carefully cut around the edge of each pita bread to make two rounds, then use a pizza cutter to cut each round into six wedges. Place the wedges on the baking sheet.
3. Brush the oil on the top of each pita wedge.
4. In a small bowl, combine the Parmesan cheese and sesame seeds.
5. Sprinkle the pita wedges with the Parmesan and sesame mixture.
6. Bake 5–10 minutes, or until light brown. Remove the baking sheet from the oven using pot holders. Use a spatula to move the pita chips from the baking sheet to a cooling rack. Let the chips cool for at least 30 minutes before eating.

PER SERVING (4 CHIPS)

Calories: 140 | Fat: 9g | Sodium: 180mg | Carbohydrates: 11g | Fiber: 0g | Sugar: 0g | Protein: 4g

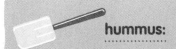

hummus:

A Middle Eastern dish that is a mixture of mashed chickpeas, garlic, and other ingredients, used especially as a dip for pita bread.

TAKE-ALONG TRAIL MIX

DIFFICULTY:
EASY

Trail mix is so versatile you can create your own versions. Try adding some yogurt-covered raisins, dry cereal, fish-shaped crackers, chocolate-coated candies, or even popcorn.

MAKES 2 CUPS

- ½ cup small pretzel sticks or twists
- ½ cup raisins
- ½ cup dry-roasted peanuts
- ¼ cup sunflower seeds
- ¼ cup semisweet chocolate chips

In a large bowl, combine all the ingredients together. Store the mixture in an airtight container or a resealable bag.

PER SERVING (½ CUP)

Calories: 320 | Fat: 19g | Sodium: 105mg | Carbohydrates: 35g | Fiber: 3g | Sugar: 22g | Protein: 8g

Chips and Dip

Fill in all the triangles to find the answer to this question:

What's the most popular dip in the United States?

Sorting the Snacks

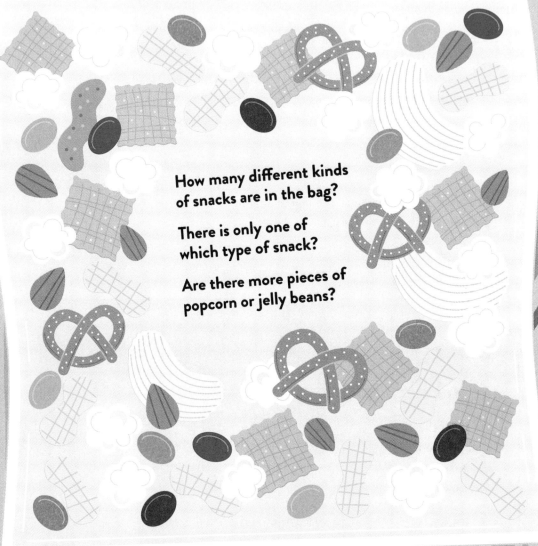

How many different kinds
of snacks are in the bag?

There is only one of
which type of snack?

Are there more pieces of
popcorn or jelly beans?

NEVER-ENOUGH NACHOS

DIFFICULTY:
MEDIUM

For a quick vegetarian version, make this without the beef. You can enjoy it as a snack with friends or even as an appetizer before a family meal.

SERVES 8

1 pound ground beef

1 cup salsa

1 medium tomato

4 scallions

1 (15-ounce) can black beans

8 ounces tortilla chips

1 cup shredded Cheddar cheese

½ cup sour cream

1 medium avocado, peeled, pitted and cut into cubes (ask an adult to help)

1. Preheat the oven to 350°F.

2. In a large skillet, cook the ground beef over medium heat for 8–10 minutes, until it is cooked throughout. Ask an adult to help you drain the extra fat from the ground beef, then place the beef in a large bowl.

3. Add the salsa and mix well with a wooden spoon.

4. Chop the tomatoes and scallions (or get an adult to help chop into small pieces). Place the tomatoes and scallions in separate small bowls. Put the black beans in a colander. Rinse and drain them and place them in a small bowl.

5. Layer the ingredients in a 9-by-13-inch baking pan in this order, starting at the bottom:

   - Tortilla chips
   - Ground beef mixture
   - Tomatoes
   - Scallions
   - Black beans
   - Shredded cheese

6. Bake 15–20 minutes, or until the cheese completely melts. Use pot holders to remove the pan from the oven. Let the nachos cool for 5 minutes, then top them with sour cream and avocado.

PER SERVING

Calories: 400 | Fat: 22g | Sodium: 790mg | Carbohydrates: 30g | Fiber: 4g | Sugar: 2g | Protein: 20g

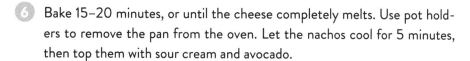

GUACAMOLE DIP

Guacamole with tortilla chips is a favorite Southwestern-style food and goes great with quesadillas, burritos, and tacos. Make sure the avocados are ripe— they should be a little soft when you lightly squeeze them, but not mushy.

SERVES 8

2 medium avocados, peeled, pitted, and mashed (ask an adult to help)

1 medium plum tomato, chopped

1 tablespoon chopped onion

1 tablespoon lime juice

1 teaspoon chopped garlic

¼ teaspoon salt

⅛ teaspoon ground black pepper

1 (13-ounce) bag tortilla chips

1. Place the avocado and chopped tomato in a medium bowl and stir to mix.
2. Add the onion, lime juice, garlic, salt, and pepper and mix.
3. Serve right away with the tortilla chips.

PER SERVING

Calories: 320 | Fat: 19g | Sodium: 320mg | Carbohydrates: 33g | Fiber: 3g | Sugar: 1g | Protein: 4g

Peel, Pit, and Mash an Avocado

Ask an adult to help you with the avocados. Carefully cut an avocado in half without cutting through the pit. Pull the two halves apart. Use a spoon to remove the pit and scoop out the insides. Put the avocado pulp in a bowl and mash it with a fork or potato masher until almost smooth.

ripe:

Fully developed and ready to be eaten.

pitted:

Without the center pit (as in peaches, olives, or avocados).

CHOCOLATE CHIP GRANOLA

Granola is fun to eat by itself, and it also makes a great topping for yogurt or ice cream.

DIFFICULTY: EASY

MAKES 5 CUPS

3½ cups rolled oats (not instant)

¼ cup vegetable oil

¼ cup honey

1 teaspoon vanilla extract

½ cup semisweet chocolate chips

½ cup white chocolate chips

½ cup sunflower seeds

½ cup slivered almonds

1. Preheat the oven to 300°F and spray a 9-by-13-inch baking pan with nonstick cooking spray.
2. In a large bowl, combine all the ingredients and mix well.
3. Spread out the granola mixture in the prepared pan.
4. Bake 15–20 minutes, or until lightly browned and heated throughout. Use pot holders to remove the pan from the oven. Place the pan on a cooling rack and let the granola cool for at least 30 minutes. Store the cooled granola in an airtight container.

PER SERVING (½ CUP)

Calories: 380 | Fat: 21g | Sodium: 40mg | Carbohydrates: 44g | Fiber: 4g | Sugar: 21g | Protein: 8g

Fun Fact

Rolled oats are rolled into flat flakes under heavy rollers. Instant oats are made from rolled oats that have been cut into smaller pieces so they cook faster.

DIFFICULTY:
EASY

QUICK S'MORES

You don't need a campfire to make this all-time favorite outdoor snack. Here's a quick version that's good any time of the year, any time of the day or night.

SERVES 2

2 large marshmallows

1 (1.55-ounce) chocolate bar, separated into 2 squares

2 graham crackers, each separated into 2 squares

1. Place a marshmallow and chocolate bar square between two graham cracker squares to make a sandwich. Repeat with the remaining ingredients to make a second sandwich.

2. Place the sandwiches on a medium microwave-safe plate and cover with a paper towel.

3. Cook for 10–15 seconds in the microwave, until the marshmallows puff and the chocolate melts slightly.

4. Carefully remove from the microwave and let cool for 20 seconds before serving.

PER SERVING

Calories: 150 | Fat: 7g | Sodium: 45mg | Carbohydrates: 22g | Fiber: 0g | Sugar: 17g | Protein: 2g

Food Trivia

S'mores were created by the Girl Scouts—the recipe for s'mores first appeared in the Girl Scout Handbook in the 1920s.

SUNNY APPLE SLICES

Instead of cream cheese, you can cover the apple slices with chocolate hazelnut spread for a sweeter snack. Add any other toppings you like—try dried fruit, chopped nuts, or candy sprinkles.

SERVES 4

1 large apple

2½ tablespoons soft cream cheese

½ cup sunflower seeds

2 teaspoons honey

1. Ask an adult to help you slice the apple into horizontal slices ½ inch thick. (Don't core the apple first.)
2. Use a mini cookie cutter (any shape you like—a circle, star, or heart would work) to cut the seeds out of the middle of each apple slice.
3. Spread about 1 teaspoon of the cream cheese over each apple slice. Sprinkle the slices with the sunflower seeds.
4. Drizzle the honey over the top. Serve the apple slices right away.

PER SERVING

Calories: 210 | Fat: 15g | Sodium: 110mg | Carbohydrates: 15g | Fiber: 3g | Sugar: 10g | Protein: 5g

Leftovers

Take a word from column B and write it next to a word in column A to make the name of a familiar food. There is more than one way to match up some words—make sure there are no leftovers!

CUP _____	FRIES
STRAW _____	MELT
POTATO _____	SAUCE
PEANUT _____	ROLL
POP _____	BURGER
CORN _____	BERRY
COLE _____	CORN
HOT _____	BUTTER
HAM _____	CAKE
FRENCH _____	SALAD
TUNA _____	SLAW
APPLE _____	CHIPS
EGG _____	DOG

YOGURT BARK

DIFFICULTY: **EASY**

No one can resist candy bark. This kind just melts in your mouth, and it's good for you too!

SERVES 6

1 (5.3-ounce) container vanilla Greek yogurt

1 tablespoon honey

¼ teaspoon vanilla extract

¼ cup granola

¼ cup blueberries or sliced strawberries

1. Line an 8-by-8-inch baking pan with parchment paper. Make sure you let some of the paper hang over the edge of the pan.

2. In a medium bowl, mix the yogurt, honey, and vanilla with a wooden spoon.

3. Spread the yogurt mixture over the parchment paper in the baking pan. Sprinkle it with the granola and berries.

4. Put the pan in the freezer for at least 4 hours. Remove the pan from the freezer and use the edges of the parchment paper to take the bark out of the pan. Break the bark into six pieces. If there are any leftovers, keep them in a covered container in the freezer.

PER SERVING

Calories: 50 | Fat: 0g | Sodium: 10mg | Carbohydrates: 10g | Fiber: 0g | Sugar: 6g | Protein: 3g

Fun Fact

Honey is the only food that never goes bad. It can last up to three thousand years without rotting!

ZUCCHINI BREAD

This sweet, tasty bread can be a snack, breakfast on the run, or even dessert. It's that good!

SERVES 10

1 large zucchini, ends trimmed and chopped

¾ cup granulated sugar

¼ cup light brown sugar

½ cup unsweetened applesauce

¼ cup vegetable oil

2 large eggs

1 teaspoon vanilla extract

2 cups all-purpose flour

½ teaspoon baking soda

½ teaspoon baking powder

½ teaspoon ground cinnamon

¼ teaspoon ground nutmeg

⅛ teaspoon salt

1. Preheat the oven to 350°F. Spray a loaf pan with nonstick cooking spray.

2. Use a blender or food processor to chop the zucchini into very small pieces. Place the zucchini in a large bowl with the granulated sugar, brown sugar, applesauce, oil, eggs, and vanilla. Use a wooden spoon to mix it. Add the flour, baking soda, baking powder, cinnamon, nutmeg, and salt and mix to combine.

3. Use a spatula to scrape the batter out of the bowl and into the pan.

4. Bake for 1 hour. Test to see if the bread is done by sticking a toothpick or skewer into the middle. If it comes out clean (with no batter stuck to it), remove it from the oven. If it's not cooked, bake it for another 5 minutes and test it again.

5. Use pot holders to remove the pan from the oven and place it on a cooling rack. Cool 15 minutes before removing it from the pan.

PER SERVING

Calories: 230 | Fat: 7g | Sodium: 135mg | Carbohydrates: 40g | Fiber: 1g | Sugar: 23g | Protein: 4g

Food Trivia

April 25 is National Zucchini Bread Day. Celebrate it with a party—and your own zucchini bread!

HONEY-ROASTED CHICKPEAS

DIFFICULTY: **MEDIUM**

When you roast chickpeas, they are as tasty and crunchy as nuts. Eat them alone or try them in a salad.

MAKES 1¼ CUPS

1 (15-ounce) can chickpeas

1 tablespoon vegetable oil

1 tablespoon light brown sugar

1 teaspoon ground cinnamon

1 teaspoon honey

1. Preheat the oven to 400°F. Line a baking sheet with parchment paper.

2. Use a can opener to open the chickpeas, then pour the chickpeas into a colander inside the sink and rinse them. Let the water drain out of the colander into the sink. Put the drained chickpeas in a medium bowl.

3. Add the oil, brown sugar, and cinnamon to the chickpeas. Stir well with a wooden spoon. Pour the chickpeas out onto the prepared baking sheet.

4. Bake for 30 minutes. Use pot holders to remove the pan from the oven and place it on a cooling rack. Drizzle the honey over the chickpeas and stir them. Use pot holders to return the pan to the oven for 5 minutes more.

5. Use pot holders again to remove the pan from the oven and place it on a cooling rack. Let the chickpeas cool completely before eating.

PER SERVING (2 TABLESPOONS)

Calories: 50 | Fat: 2g | Sodium: 95mg | Carbohydrates: 8g | Fiber: 1g | Sugar: 3g | Protein: 2g

PARMESAN EDAMAME

Have you ever eaten edamame in a Japanese restaurant? They're fun to pop out of their shells and into your mouth. This recipe uses frozen edamame, which is already out of the shell.

MAKES 1 CUP

1 cup frozen shelled edamame, thawed

1 tablespoon vegetable oil

3 tablespoons grated Parmesan cheese, divided

¼ teaspoon salt

¼ teaspoon ground black pepper

① Preheat the oven to 400°F. Line a baking sheet with parchment paper.

② Place the edamame in a colander in the sink and rinse them. Let the water drain out of the colander into the sink. Put the drained edamame in a medium bowl. Pat dry with paper towels.

③ Add the oil, 2 tablespoons of the cheese, and the salt and pepper to the edamame in the bowl. Stir well with a wooden spoon. Pour the edamame out onto the prepared baking sheet in a single layer.

④ Bake for 15–20 minutes or until the edamame is lightly golden brown. Using pot holders, remove the pan from the oven and place it on a cooling rack.

⑤ Let the edamame cool for at least 30 minutes. Before serving, sprinkle with the remaining 1 tablespoon of the cheese.

PER SERVING (2 TABLESPOONS)

Calories: 50 | Fat: 3.5g | Sodium: 125mg | Carbohydrates: 2g | Fiber: 1g | Sugar: 0g | Protein: 3g

Chapter 5

WHAT'S FOR DINNER?

Many families try to spend mealtime together—it's the one time during the day when everyone can be in the same place! Eating together as a family, even for just a short time, is better for kids, and even helps them achieve better grades. WOW!

LAZY RAVIOLI LASAGNA

This dinner is so good and so much fun to make! If you want to add some vegetables to this casserole, add 1 cup chopped vegetables or 2 cups baby spinach leaves to the sauce.

SERVES 8

1 (24-ounce) jar marinara pasta sauce

1 (20-ounce) package refrigerated cheese ravioli

1 teaspoon dried oregano

1 teaspoon dried basil

2 cups shredded mozzarella cheese

2 tablespoons grated Parmesan cheese

1. Preheat the oven to 400°F. Spray a 9-by-13-inch baking pan with nonstick cooking spray.

2. Spread 1 cup of the pasta sauce over the bottom of the pan. Arrange half of the ravioli over the pasta sauce. Sprinkle with half of the oregano and basil.

3. Spread the rest of the pasta sauce over the ravioli. Top with the rest of the ravioli, oregano, and basil.

4. Sprinkle the mozzarella and Parmesan cheeses over the top.

5. Cover the dish loosely with a piece of foil. (Spray the foil on the inside with nonstick cooking spray to keep it from sticking to the cheese.)

6. Bake the lasagna for 30 minutes. Use pot holders to take the pan out of the oven. Carefully remove the foil and put the pan back in the oven. Bake for another 10 minutes.

7. Remove the pan from the oven using pot holders and place it on a cooling rack. (Or have an adult help you.) Let the lasagna cool for 10–15 minutes before cutting the lasagna into eight pieces. Use a spatula to remove the pieces from the pan.

PER SERVING

Calories: 370 | Fat: 17g | Sodium: 910mg | Carbohydrates: 36g | Fiber: 2g | Sugar: 6g | Protein: 19g

PARMESAN CHICKEN FINGERS

Making your own chicken fingers is so easy, you will wonder why you didn't try to make them before. And this recipe lets you add some Parmesan cheese to make them even tastier.

SERVES 6

1 pound chicken tenders

1 large egg

¼ cup milk

3 tablespoons vegetable oil, divided

1 tablespoon water

½ cup bread crumbs

¼ cup grated Parmesan cheese

2 tablespoons all-purpose flour

½ teaspoon salt

¼ teaspoon ground black pepper

1. Place the chicken tenders in a large bowl.
2. In a small bowl, mix together the egg, the milk, 1 tablespoon of the oil, and the water with a whisk. Pour the mixture over the chicken.
3. On a large plate, mix the bread crumbs, cheese, flour, salt, and pepper.
4. Remove the chicken tenders from the bowl and dip them into the bread crumb mixture, coating evenly. Place on a clean plate.
5. In a large skillet, heat the remaining 2 tablespoons of the oil over medium heat. Cook the chicken fingers until they are lightly browned on one side, about 5–7 minutes. Use tongs to turn the tenders and cook the other side until browned, about 3–5 minutes.
6. Use the tongs to put the chicken on a clean plate. Serve warm.

PER SERVING

Calories: 340 | Fat: 22g | Sodium: 750mg | Carbohydrates: 20g | Fiber: 0g | Sugar: 2g | Protein: 16g

Make Your Own

Make your own crumbs by putting corn flakes or toasted, dried bread in a resealable bag and smashing them with a rolling pin until they are all crumbs.

SLOPPY JOES

To make these easier—and less messy—to eat, scoop out a small amount of bread from the bun to make a bowl. Put the Sloppy Joe mixture in the bread bowl and top with the other half of the bun. It works!

DIFFICULTY: **MEDIUM**

SERVES 8

1 tablespoon vegetable oil

1 small onion, peeled and chopped

1 pound ground beef

2 cups frozen hash brown potatoes, thawed

1 (15-ounce) can Sloppy Joe sauce

8 hamburger buns

1. Heat the oil in a large skillet over medium heat. Add the onion to the skillet and cook, stirring with a wooden spoon, for 5 minutes.

2. Add the ground beef and use the wooden spoon to break up the meat and stir while cooking until the meat is brown and no longer pink, about 8 minutes. Ask an adult to help you drain the extra fat from the ground beef.

3. Add the hash brown potatoes to the skillet and stir to mix. Use a can opener to open the Sloppy Joe sauce, then pour the sauce over the top and stir again to mix everything together. Cover the skillet.

4. Reduce the heat to low and simmer for 30 minutes. Use a large spoon to scoop the Sloppy Joe mixture onto the hamburger buns and serve right away.

PER SERVING

Calories: 340 | Fat: 11g | Sodium: 1,080mg | Carbohydrates: 34g | Fiber: 1g | Sugar: 12g | Protein: 20g

Handling Leftovers

Keep leftovers in a bowl sealed tightly with plastic wrap or in airtight containers. Promptly store them in the freezer or refrigerator.

DIFFICULTY: EASY

CHICKEN QUESADILLAS WITH SALSA

This recipe is easy enough that you will be able to make it for yourself and your family. Try it with some sour cream and Guacamole Dip (Chapter 4) spooned on top.

SERVES 4

4 (8-inch) flour tortillas

½ cup chopped cooked chicken breast

¼ cup shredded Cheddar cheese

2 tablespoons salsa

1. Place one tortilla on a microwave-safe dinner plate.
2. Top with half of the cooked chicken, half of the cheese, and half of the salsa. Place another tortilla on top.
3. Heat the quesadilla in the microwave for 15–20 seconds, or until the cheese melts. Remove from the microwave and cool slightly, then cut into wedges.
4. Repeat with the remaining ingredients.

PER SERVING

Calories: 210 | Fat: 7g | Sodium: 630mg | Carbohydrates: 26g | Fiber: 0g | Sugar: 1g | Protein: 11g

Fun Fact

The word *quesadilla* means "little cheesy thing" in Spanish, and people in northern and central Mexico have been making and eating them since the sixteenth century.

ORANGE CHICKEN

DIFFICULTY:
MEDIUM

The orange juice, butter, and brown sugar make a tasty sweet sauce for the chicken. You can try the sauce with fish too.

SERVES 4

4 (5-ounce) boneless, skinless chicken breasts

4 teaspoons Dijon mustard

2 scallions, chopped

¾ cup orange juice

1 tablespoon butter, cut into 4 small pieces

4 tablespoons light brown sugar

1. Preheat the oven to 350°F.
2. Place the chicken in a 9-by-13-inch baking pan.
3. Spread the mustard evenly over the chicken breasts. Sprinkle with the scallions.
4. Pour the orange juice into the dish around and over the chicken.
5. Top each chicken breast with a piece of butter and sprinkle with the brown sugar.
6. Bake uncovered for 30–35 minutes, or until the chicken is fully cooked. Use pot holders to remove the pan from the oven. Serve right away.

PER SERVING

Calories: 280 | Fat: 7g | Sodium: 190mg | Carbohydrates: 19g | Fiber: 0g | Sugar: 17g | Protein: 32g

How to Tell If Chicken Is Done

To test for doneness, cut into the chicken and see if the chicken is white on the inside. If there is any pink, the chicken is not fully cooked and needs to go back in the oven for a few more minutes.

TERIYAKI SALMON PACKS

It's fun to make dinner in a package—it's like giving everyone a gift to open! And it's easy to clean up too!

SERVES 4

3 tablespoons light brown sugar

3 tablespoons soy sauce

1½ tablespoons rice wine vinegar

2 cloves garlic, peeled and minced

¼ teaspoon salt

¼ teaspoon ground black pepper

4 (4-ounce) salmon fillets

1 teaspoon cornstarch

1 tablespoon sesame seeds

1. Put the brown sugar, soy sauce, rice vinegar, garlic, salt, and pepper in a medium microwave-safe bowl to make the marinade. Mix with a whisk.

2. Place the salmon fillets in a large zip-top bag. Pour half of the marinade into the bag and seal it, squeezing out any excess air. Keep the remaining marinade in the bowl. Turn the bag over a few times to get the marinade all around the salmon. Place the bag in the refrigerator and let it marinate for 30 minutes to 1 hour.

3. Preheat the oven to 400°F. Tear four large pieces of foil, each about 10 inches square.

4. Using tongs, carefully remove the salmon from the marinade and place one salmon fillet on each piece of foil. Wrap the foil loosely around the salmon, and place the salmon packets on a baking sheet.

5. Put the baking sheet in the oven and bake for 20–25 minutes until the salmon is browned on top and flakes easily when pricked with a fork. Use pot holders to remove the salmon from the oven. (Be careful when checking for doneness—the steam will be hot!)

6. To make the sauce, add the cornstarch to the rest of the marinade in the bowl. Whisk it together until it's smooth. Put the bowl in the microwave and heat on high for 20 seconds. Carefully remove the bowl from the microwave and stir.

7 Open the foil packets about a quarter of the way, drizzle the sauce over the salmon, and sprinkle with the sesame seeds. Move the packets to four plates and serve.

PER SERVING

Calories: 300 | Fat: 16g | Sodium: 1,180mg | Carbohydrates: 14g | Fiber: 0g | Sugar: 13g | Protein: 24g

marinate:

To soak meat, fish, or other foods in a liquid mixture before cooking. The liquid adds flavor to the food and sometimes makes the food (usually meats) more tender.

Oodles of Noodles

Follow the strands of linguine over and under to see which kid gets which meatball.

CHEESE-CRUSTED FISH FILLETS

You can start with either frozen or fresh fish fillets. Cod, tilapia, haddock, or any other type of whitefish can be used in this dish.

SERVES 4

4 (4-ounce) whitefish fillets, like tilapia or cod

4 ounces cream cheese, softened

1 garlic clove, peeled and minced

2 scallions, chopped

1 teaspoon lemon juice

1 tablespoon chopped fresh parsley

1. Preheat the oven to 350°F. Spray a 9-by-13-inch baking pan with non-stick cooking spray.
2. Lay the fish fillets in a single layer in the baking pan.
3. In a small bowl, combine the cream cheese, garlic, scallions, and lemon juice. Mix well with a wooden spoon.
4. Spread the cream cheese mixture over the top of each fish fillet.
5. Bake for 15–20 minutes, or until the fish is lightly browned on top and fully cooked. Use pot holders to remove the pan from the oven. Sprinkle the fillets with the parsley before serving.

PER SERVING

Calories: 200 | Fat: 10g | Sodium: 180mg | Carbohydrates: 3g | Fiber: 0g | Sugar: 2g | Protein: 25g

Testing Fish

You have to test baked fish to make sure it's done. With a fork, pick off a piece from the end of the fish when you think it might be done cooking. If the fish flakes off easily, it's done. If it doesn't come off easily, cook it for a few minutes longer and repeat the process.

BITE-SIZED PIZZAS

Here's a super easy and quick way to make pizza. Experiment with different toppings, like slices of pepperoni or chopped vegetables.

DIFFICULTY:
EASY

SERVES 8

1 (16.3-ounce) can refrigerated biscuits

¾ cup pasta sauce

1 cup shredded mozzarella cheese

1. Preheat the oven to 375°F.
2. Open the biscuit can and separate the biscuits.
3. Place the biscuits on a large baking sheet. Press down on the biscuits to flatten them.
4. Using a large spoon, spread some of the pasta sauce over each biscuit. Top each with the cheese.
5. Bake pizzas for 8–10 minutes, or until crusts are golden brown and the cheese is melted. Use pot holders to remove the baking sheet from the oven. Serve hot.

PER SERVING

Calories: 200 | Fat: 7g | Sodium: 620mg | Carbohydrates: 28g | Fiber: 0g | Sugar: 4g | Protein: 7g

Play It Safe

Pot holders or oven mitts are a necessity in every kitchen. Make sure you have both hands covered before touching any hot foods in the oven or on the stovetop.

TASTY TACOS

Everyone loves tacos! And best of all, everyone can put their own taco together. Add some Guacamole Dip (Chapter 4) and sour cream to the toppings if you like.

SERVES 8

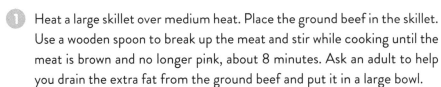

1 pound ground beef

1 (1-ounce) packet taco
   seasoning

2 tablespoons water

1 large tomato, chopped

1 cup chopped lettuce

½ cup shredded Cheddar cheese

½ cup salsa

8 hard taco shells

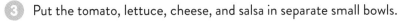

1. Heat a large skillet over medium heat. Place the ground beef in the skillet. Use a wooden spoon to break up the meat and stir while cooking until the meat is brown and no longer pink, about 8 minutes. Ask an adult to help you drain the extra fat from the ground beef and put it in a large bowl.

2. Add the taco seasoning and water to the ground beef and stir it together to mix.

3. Put the tomato, lettuce, cheese, and salsa in separate small bowls.

4. Put all the bowls on the table with the taco shells and let your guests create their own tacos.

PER SERVING

Calories: 240 | Fat: 13g | Sodium: 730mg | Carbohydrates: 12g | Fiber: 2g | Sugar: 2g | Protein: 17g

Play It Safe

Be sure to wash your hands with soap and water before touching food. It is also important to wash your hands right after you handle raw meat or fish and before you touch other things.

FETTUCCINE ALFREDO WITH CHICKEN

It's no secret that kids love pasta with Alfredo sauce (which is just another way of saying "mac and cheese"). Here's an easy way to make it at home.

SERVES 4

½ pound uncooked fettuccine

2 (5-ounce) boneless, skinless chicken breasts

¼ cup half-and-half

½ cup evaporated skim milk

2 tablespoons butter

¾ cup grated Parmesan cheese

1. Pour water into a medium pot until it is two-thirds full. Place the pot over high heat and bring the water to a boil. Add the fettuccine and cook it for 10 minutes, stirring occasionally. Place a colander in the sink and ask an adult to help you carefully pour the pasta and water into the colander to drain.

2. While the pasta is cooking, spray a medium skillet with nonstick cooking spray and place it over medium heat. Cook the chicken breasts until done, 7–9 minutes on each side. Use tongs to move the chicken from the pan to a cutting board. Cool for 10 minutes, then cut it up into thin strips. Set aside.

3. In a large saucepan, combine the half-and-half, milk, and butter. Heat over medium heat until the butter is melted and the mixture is hot. Slowly add in the cheese.

4. Reduce the heat to low and cook, stirring with a wooden spoon, until the mixture is thick.

5. Stir in the fettuccine and the chicken and mix well. Serve right away.

PER SERVING

Calories: 470 | Fat: 16g | Sodium: 420mg | Carbohydrates: 47g | Fiber: 0g | Sugar: 7g | Protein: 35g

Play It Safe

Know how to use the various appliances and utensils you will need. If you need to, ask an adult to teach or remind you how they work. Always have an adult with you whenever you use anything that is sharp (like a knife or food processor) or hot (like a skillet on a stove or a pan in the oven).

QUICK AND EASY CHILI

DIFFICULTY:
MEDIUM

If you like a spicier chili, use diced tomatoes with chilies added. There are lots of toppings you could use along with the cheese and sour cream. Put out small bowls of things like chopped onion, diced avocado, olives, or even cooked pasta so everyone can make their own bowl the way they like it.

SERVES 6

1 pound ground beef or ground turkey

1 small onion, peeled and chopped

1 (15-ounce) can kidney beans

2 (15-ounce) cans diced tomatoes, undrained

2 teaspoons chili powder

1 cup shredded Cheddar cheese

½ cup sour cream

1. Put a large saucepan or Dutch oven on the stove over medium-high heat. Cook the ground beef and onion for 5–10 minutes until the beef is browned and the onion is translucent (you can almost see through it). Stir the beef with a wooden spoon to help break it up. Ask an adult help you drain any extra fat from the pan.

2. Use a can opener to open the beans and tomatoes. Drain the beans in a colander in the sink. Run water over them to rinse them and drain well. Add the beans, tomatoes, and chili powder to the saucepan. Increase the heat to high until the mixture starts boiling, then reduce the heat to low.

3. Cover the saucepan and simmer for 20 minutes. (Much of the liquid will evaporate, allowing the chili to get thicker.)

4. Serve the chili in bowls, topped with the cheese and sour cream.

PER SERVING

Calories: 400 | Fat: 21g | Sodium: 930mg | Carbohydrates: 21g | Fiber: 6g | Sugar: 6g | Protein: 29g

Chef Andrew

Andrew has cooked his very first meal all by himself. What did he make? Use the picture and letter equations to sound out the answers.

B+   -R   +D   +NZ

 C+    SL+   -P

 +S

T

Kiss the Cook

This cook has eaten so many vegetables and salads that he has turned quite green! Connect the dots to see his picture.

Finishing Touches:
Draw a circle around the one dot that has no number.
Then, color in the cook's picture.

Chapter 6

EAT ALL THE COLORS

Eating fruits and vegetables every day helps round out your meals and gives you the nutrition you need to stay healthy. When you choose a vegetable or a fruit, think about all the different colors to choose from—the more colorful you make your plate, the more nutrients you are adding to your overall diet. Choose some orange (carrots, sweet potatoes, apricots, or cantaloupe), red (red bell peppers, tomatoes, cherries, or strawberries), green (broccoli, lettuce, or spinach), and blue and purple (blueberries or grapes) to help you grow and stay healthy. See how many different choices and colors you can find.

ROASTED BRUSSELS SPROUTS WITH CRANBERRIES

If you've never tried Brussels sprouts, you might be surprised at how tasty they are when you roast them. The cranberries add a little burst of sweet-tart flavor.

SERVES 4

1 pound small Brussels sprouts

1 tablespoon olive oil

½ teaspoon salt

¼ cup dried cranberries

1. Preheat the oven to 425°F.
2. Trim the ends and outer leaves from the Brussels sprouts and place them in a colander in the sink. Run cool water over the sprouts. Drain them, then dry them off with paper towels. Put the Brussels sprouts in a medium bowl.
3. Add the oil and salt to the Brussels sprouts. Mix well using a wooden spoon. Spread the sprouts in a single layer on a large baking sheet.
4. Roast for 20–25 minutes until the Brussels sprouts are browned and crispy around the edges. Use pot holders to carefully remove the pan from the oven.
5. Use a spatula to move the Brussels sprouts to a serving bowl. Add the cranberries and stir. Serve right away.

PER SERVING

Calories: 110 | Fat: 4g | Sodium: 320mg | Carbohydrates: 18g | Fiber: 5g | Sugar: 10g | Protein: 4g

Fun Fact

Brussels sprouts grow in a cluster up and down thick, woody stalks. The stalks can grow to almost 4 feet high!

CLASSIC CAESAR SALAD

DIFFICULTY:
EASY

Caesar salad is light and fresh. You can add chicken or shrimp to make it a meal by itself, or eat it with a simple dinner like grilled steak or an Italian dish like Fettuccine Alfredo with Chicken (Chapter 5).

SERVES 2

1 small head romaine lettuce

2 tablespoons shredded Parmesan cheese

½ cup croutons

¼ cup bottled Caesar salad dressing

1. Separate the leaves from the head of lettuce and rinse them under running water. Lay the leaves out to dry on paper towels.

2. Tear the lettuce into small pieces and place the pieces in a large bowl.

3. Top the lettuce with the cheese and croutons.

4. Pour the dressing over the salad. Use tongs or two large forks to toss the salad around in the bowl until the lettuce is coated with dressing. Serve right away.

PER SERVING

Calories: 220 | Fat: 18g | Sodium: 520mg | Carbohydrates: 10g | Fiber: 1g | Sugar: 3g | Protein: 5g

Food Trivia

Lettuce is the second most popular fresh vegetable in the United States. The most popular one? Potatoes, of course!

LEMON AND HONEY SALAD DRESSING

This dressing is delicious on a green salad. You could also use it as a sauce to pour over baked chicken or fish.

MAKES ½ CUP

¼ cup lemon juice

⅓ cup honey

¼ teaspoon ground nutmeg

¼ teaspoon salt

1. Mix the lemon juice and honey in a small bowl with a whisk. Add the nutmeg and salt and continue to whisk everything together.

2. Use the dressing right away or store it in the refrigerator until you're ready to use it.

PER SERVING (2 TABLESPOONS)

Calories: 90 | Fat: 0g | Sodium: 150mg | Carbohydrates: 24g | Fiber: 0g | Sugar: 21g | Protein: 0g

Hidden Veggies

Find five vegetables from the list hiding in the sentences.

1. Chop each carrot very carefully!

2. Abe answered, "I love lettuce!"

3. Can you spin a cherry?

4. Fill the cab! Bag each vegetable!

5. The bee tasted the broccoli.

TOMATO
SPINACH
PEPPER
CABBAGE
CELERY
TURNIP
PEA
BEAN
BEET

GREEN BEANS WITH ALMONDS

There's nothing like the fresh, crisp sound of snapping beans. This recipe is not only fun and easy to make, but also crunchy and healthy to eat.

DIFFICULTY:
EASY

SERVES 4

½ pound fresh green beans

1 tablespoon butter

¼ cup slivered almonds

½ teaspoon salt

¼ teaspoon ground pepper

1. Trim the beans by snapping off the ends and removing any loose strings, then use a colander to hold the beans while you rinse them in cool water.

2. In a large saucepan, heat 2 quarts of water over high heat until it boils.

3. Add the beans to the boiling water. Cook them for about 5 minutes, until they are slightly tender but still crisp.

4. Ask an adult to help you drain the green beans in the colander. Return them to the saucepan.

5. Add the butter, almonds, salt, and pepper. Mix everything together with a wooden spoon until the butter is melted and the green beans are evenly covered with butter. Serve warm.

PER SERVING

Calories: 80 | Fat: 6g | Sodium: 300mg |
Carbohydrates: 6g | Fiber: 2g | Sugar: 2g |
Protein: 3g

Grow Your Own

Visit a local farm or, better yet, plant some string bean plants in your backyard garden. You can watch the string beans grow and pick them yourself. Then, you can add your own homegrown string beans to dinner.

SWEET BABY CARROTS

Baby-cut carrots are made from full-sized carrots, but they're peeled and cut into smaller pieces to make them easier to eat. You can enjoy them raw or cooked.

SERVES 4

1 pound baby-cut carrots

1 tablespoon butter

2 tablespoons light brown sugar

1. In a large saucepan, combine the carrots and just enough water to cover them.
2. Put the saucepan over high heat until the water begins to boil.
3. Reduce the heat to medium and continue cooking until the carrots are slightly soft, about 15 minutes.
4. Ask an adult to help you drain the carrots in a colander. Return them to the saucepan.
5. Add the butter and brown sugar to the saucepan, stirring with a wooden spoon until the butter is melted and the carrots are covered with the butter. Serve warm.

PER SERVING

Calories: 90 | Fat: 3g | Sodium: 90mg | Carbohydrates: 16g | Fiber: 3g | Sugar: 12g | Protein: 1g

Surprise Salad

Find eleven items in Rebecca's salad before they get eaten!

BICYCLE

KITE

BALLOON

BELL

HEART

SAILBOAT

MITTEN

CROWN

GHOST

DIAMOND RING

CHRISTMAS TREE

SWEET POTATO CASSEROLE

DIFFICULTY: **MEDIUM**

This sweet side dish can be made for the holidays as a special treat or just as a delicious side dish during the week.

SERVES 6

1 (29-ounce) can sweet potatoes in light syrup

1½ cups mini marshmallows, divided

¼ cup melted butter

¼ cup orange juice

½ teaspoon ground cinnamon

1. Preheat the oven to 350°F.

2. Use a can opener to open the can of sweet potatoes. Place a colander in the sink and pour in the sweet potatoes to drain. Put the drained sweet potatoes in a large bowl, then mash them with a potato masher or fork until they are mostly smooth.

3. Add 1 cup of the marshmallows, the butter, the orange juice, and the cinnamon. Gently mix them together with a wooden spoon.

4. Pour the mixture into a 1-quart casserole dish.

5. Bake for 20 minutes. Use pot holders to remove the casserole dish from the oven.

6. Sprinkle the remaining ½ cup of the marshmallows over the top of the casserole and, using pot holders, return it to the oven for 5 minutes longer.

7. Remove the dish from the oven using pot holders and let cool for 10 minutes before serving.

PER SERVING

Calories: 250 | Fat: 8g | Sodium: 45mg | Carbohydrates: 43g | Fiber: 2g | Sugar: 22g | Protein: 3g

Fun Fact

Sweet potatoes had been grown in South and Central America for five thousand years before Christopher Columbus arrived. He brought some back to Spain and introduced them to the people of Europe.

BOW TIE PASTA PRIMAVERA

DIFFICULTY:
MEDIUM

If you don't have bow tie–shaped pasta, you can make this dish with any shape of pasta you like. Add whatever fresh vegetables you like too. (Primavera is the word for "spring" in Italian; it's also used in names of dishes made with vegetables.)

SERVES 6

12 ounces bow tie pasta

1 tablespoon salt

1 small zucchini

1 small yellow squash

1 medium red bell pepper

1 tablespoon olive oil

⅓ cup prepared pesto sauce

2 tablespoons grated Parmesan cheese

1. Pour water into a large saucepan or pot until it is two-thirds full. Place the pot over high heat and bring the water to a boil. Add the pasta and the salt and cook for 10 minutes, stirring occasionally. Place a colander in the sink and ask an adult to help you pour the pasta and water into the colander to drain.

2. While the pasta cooks, chop the vegetables. Trim the stem ends of the zucchini and yellow squash and cut them into small pieces. Cut the bell pepper in half, remove the seeds and stem, and cut into small pieces.

3. Heat the oil in a large skillet over medium-high heat. Use tongs to stir-fry the vegetables until they are tender-crisp, about 8 minutes.

4. Add the pesto sauce and stir to mix. Remove the skillet from the heat and stir in the pasta. Top with the cheese and serve.

Pasta Shapes

There are more than six hundred different shapes of pasta made throughout the world. Most types of pasta we eat today were first made in Italy. The Italians usually named pasta shapes for things they look like, including *spaghetti* (little strings), *campanelle* (bells), *conchiglie* (shells), *linguine* (little tongues), *fettuccine* (little ribbons), and *vermicelli* (little worms). The name in Italian for bow tie pasta is *farfalle*, which means "butterfly."

PER SERVING

Calories: 330 | Fat: 12g | Sodium: 1,350mg | Carbohydrates: 45g | Fiber: 1g | Sugar: 4g | Protein: 10g

DIFFICULTY:
HARD

VEGGIE LASAGNA

Try other vegetables in your lasagna as well—zucchini, yellow squash, eggplant, spinach, shredded carrots—there are so many options!

SERVES 6

1 large egg	6 no-bake lasagna noodles
1 cup ricotta cheese	½ cup finely chopped broccoli
1 cup shredded mozzarella cheese, divided	½ cup finely chopped red bell pepper
1 cup pasta sauce	½ cup finely chopped mushrooms

1. Preheat the oven to 375°F. Spray a 9-inch square baking pan with nonstick cooking spray.

2. Use a whisk to beat the egg in a medium bowl. Add the ricotta cheese and ½ cup of the mozzarella cheese. Mix well with a wooden spoon.

3. Spread ⅓ cup of sauce on the bottom of the prepared pan. Top with two lasagna noodles side by side. Spread a third of the cheese mixture on top of the noodles. Sprinkle a third of the vegetables on top, then add another ⅓ cup of sauce.

4. Continue layering with two more noodles, another third of the cheese mixture, another third of the vegetables, and the last ⅓ cup of the pasta sauce.

5. Finish the layers with the last two noodles, the last third of the cheese mixture, and the last third of the vegetables. Sprinkle the remaining ½ cup of mozzarella on top.

6. Cover the pan with foil. Bake for 40–45 minutes, or until hot and bubbly.

7. Use pot holders or oven mitts to remove the foil from the pan. Bake the lasagna for an additional 5 minutes to brown the cheese on top.

8. Use pot holders to remove the pan from the oven. Let the lasagna cool for about 10–15 minutes before cutting and serving it.

PER SERVING

Calories: 250 | Fat: 11g | Sodium: 330mg | Carbohydrates: 26g | Fiber: 0g | Sugar: 6g | Protein: 15g

FRUITY RICE

The apples and dried fruit make this rice a nice autumn dish. Try it with ham or Teriyaki Salmon Packs (Chapter 5).

DIFFICULTY:
MEDIUM

SERVES 4

1 cup uncooked long-grain rice

2 cups water

2 medium apples

1 tablespoon vegetable oil

¼ cup raisins

¼ cup dried cranberries

1. Add the rice and water to a medium saucepan. Cook over high heat until the mixture boils. Reduce the heat to low, cover the pan, and simmer for 20–25 minutes, or until all the water is absorbed. Set aside.

2. Use a corer to remove the cores from the apples, then chop them into small pieces, leaving the apple skin on. (If you don't have an apple corer, ask an adult to help you cut around the core.)

3. Heat the oil in a small skillet over medium heat. Add the apples and cook for about 5 minutes, while you stir them around with a wooden spoon.

4. Stir in the raisins, dried cranberries, and rice.

5. Continue cooking and stirring for 10 minutes, or until the mixture is heated throughout. Serve warm.

PER SERVING

Calories: 230 | Fat: 4g | Sodium: 0mg | Carbohydrates: 49g | Fiber: 3g | Sugar: 21g | Protein: 2g

A Native American Fruit

Native Americans were the first to harvest and eat tart cranberries. They mixed dried deer meat and mashed cranberries to make pemmican, a food that provided energy and could be kept for a long time. Native Americans also used cranberry juice as a natural dye for clothes and blankets.

BROCCOLI-STUFFED BAKED POTATO

Try stuffing your potato with other vegetables you like too. Mushrooms, spinach, and bell peppers are all good choices.

SERVES 1

1 large russet potato

1 teaspoon butter

¼ cup chopped fresh or frozen broccoli

1 teaspoon water

¼ cup shredded Cheddar cheese

1. Poke about four holes in the potato using a paring knife. Place it on a microwave-safe plate.

2. Cook the potato in the microwave on high for 5 minutes. Turn the potato over and continue to cook for 5 more minutes. Use pot holders to remove the plate from the microwave.

3. Cut the potato open wide and top it with the butter. Set it aside for a minute.

4. Place the broccoli and water in a small microwave-safe bowl and cook it in the microwave on high for 2 minutes. Remove the bowl from the microwave and pour the broccoli into a colander to drain.

5. Mash up the inside of the potato a little with a fork. Top the potato with the broccoli. Sprinkle the cheese on top of the broccoli. Place the stuffed potato in the microwave again and heat for 30 seconds to 1 minute on high, until the cheese is melted. Carefully remove the plate from the microwave and let it cool for 1–2 minutes before eating.

PER SERVING

Calories: 290 | Fat: 10g | Sodium: 250mg | Carbohydrates: 41g | Fiber: 3g | Sugar: 2g | Protein: 12g

paring knife:

A knife with a small blade, used to peel or cut small foods.

RAINBOW COLESLAW

This colorful slaw is great with sandwiches, burgers, or grilled chicken, and perfect for a backyard barbecue.

SERVES 4

1 small green bell pepper

1 small red bell pepper

1 (16-ounce) package coleslaw mix with carrots

6 tablespoons apple cider vinegar

¼ cup sugar

3 tablespoons vegetable oil

2 tablespoons water

1. Cut the bell peppers in half and remove the seeds and stem. Cut the peppers into very thin slices.

2. In a large bowl, combine the coleslaw mix and sliced peppers.

3. In a small bowl, combine the vinegar, sugar, oil, and water. Mix well with a whisk.

4. Pour the vinegar mixture over the vegetables and stir with a wooden spoon. Serve right away or cover the bowl and refrigerate the coleslaw for up to one day.

PER SERVING

Calories: 180 | Fat: 11g | Sodium: 30mg | Carbohydrates: 22g | Fiber: 4g | Sugar: 18g | Protein: 2g

Fun Fact

Red bell peppers are green bell peppers that have been left on the vine longer and have continued to ripen.

PARMESAN POTATO FRIES

You can prepare these potatoes with or without the skin in whatever shape you like. Before you know it, they'll be a favorite at your family's dinner table.

SERVES 4

4 small potatoes

2 tablespoons vegetable oil

1 teaspoon salt

½ teaspoon ground black pepper

1 tablespoon grated Parmesan cheese

1. Preheat the oven to 350°F. Spray a large baking sheet with nonstick cooking spray. Cut the potatoes into strips or rounds or any shape you choose.

2. Put the potatoes in a large bowl. Add the oil and stir with a wooden spoon until the potatoes are coated with the oil. Sprinkle the potatoes with the salt, pepper, and cheese. Stir again.

3. Place the potatoes in a single layer on the prepared baking sheet. Bake for 25 minutes. Use pot holders to remove the baking sheet from the oven. Carefully flip the potatoes over with a spatula and, using pot holders, return the baking sheet to the oven. Bake for 20 minutes more until the potatoes are crispy and golden brown.

4. Use pot holders to remove the baking sheet from the oven. Serve hot.

Try This

Cut up two potatoes. Put one into a pot full of water. Leave the other out on the counter. What did you notice about the two potatoes? The one in the water didn't get brown, but the one on the counter did. Why? Because once you cut a potato, you expose its cells to the oxygen in the air, which causes the potato to brown. If you put the potato in water, the oxygen cannot reach the cells, so the potato doesn't brown.

PER SERVING

Calories: 200 | Fat: 8g | Sodium: 630mg | Carbohydrates: 30g | Fiber: 4g | Sugar: 1g | Protein: 4g

VEGETABLE TORTILLA SOUP

Make this as mild or as spicy as you wish by adding more or less hot sauce, depending on what you and your guests or family like.

SERVES 4

1 tablespoon vegetable oil

1 small onion, peeled and chopped

1 tablespoon tomato paste

½ teaspoon ground cumin

¼ teaspoon chili powder

2 small tomatoes, chopped

¼ cup chopped green pepper

¼ cup chopped red pepper

1 tablespoon lime juice

4 cups vegetable or chicken broth

½ cup canned black beans, rinsed and drained

½ cup frozen corn kernels

½ teaspoon salt

⅛ teaspoon ground black pepper

⅛ teaspoon hot pepper sauce

1 large ripe avocado, peeled, pitted, and chopped (ask an adult to help)

¼ cup shredded Cheddar cheese

4 ounces tortilla chips

1. Heat the oil in a large saucepan or Dutch oven over medium heat. Add the onion and cook for about 5 minutes, stirring often with a wooden spoon. Add tomato paste, cumin, and chili powder and cook for 30 seconds.

2. Add the tomatoes and bell peppers. Cook for about 2 minutes, until the vegetables are softened. Stir in the lime juice, broth, beans, corn, salt, black pepper, and hot pepper sauce. When the soup boils, turn the heat down to low. Simmer the soup for 10 minutes.

3. Use a ladle to pour the soup into individual bowls. Top each bowl with avocado, cheese, and tortilla chips. Serve right away.

PER SERVING

Calories: 340 | Fat: 18g | Sodium: 1,310mg | Carbohydrates: 40g | Fiber: 7g | Sugar: 9g | Protein: 8g

Dutch oven:

A large, heavy pot with a tight-fitting domed cover good for making large quantities of soup, chili, and pasta.

DIFFICULTY:
MEDIUM

FRIED QUINOA

Here's a different way to make fried rice—without the rice!

SERVES 8

1 cup uncooked white or red quinoa

2 cups water

1 teaspoon vegetable oil

1 small onion, peeled and chopped

1 (8-ounce) bag frozen shelled edamame

½ cup shredded carrots

2 tablespoons soy sauce

2 large eggs

½ teaspoon salt

¼ teaspoon ground black pepper

1. Put the quinoa in a fine-mesh strainer or colander and rinse it under cold water. Put the quinoa in a medium saucepan. Add the water.

2. Heat the saucepan over medium-high heat until the mixture starts to boil, then reduce the heat to medium-low and cover the saucepan. Simmer for 12–15 minutes until the quinoa has soaked up all the water.

3. Heat the oil in a large skillet over medium-high heat. Add the onion and sauté for 3 minutes until tender. Add the edamame and carrots. Cook and stir for 3 minutes more. Stir in the soy sauce.

4. Crack the eggs into a small bowl and lightly beat them with a fork.

5. Use the spatula to slide the vegetables to one side of the skillet. Pour the eggs into the empty side and cook for 2 minutes, stirring.

6. Add the quinoa and stir with a wooden spoon. Season with salt and pepper. Serve warm.

PER SERVING

Calories: 150 | Fat: 3.5g | Sodium: 470mg | Carbohydrates: 21g | Fiber: 3g | Sugar: 3g | Protein: 8g

fine-mesh strainer:

A strainer with very small holes that can be used to strain or rinse foods that are very small, like quinoa or rice.

BROCCOLI AND CHEESE-STUFFED SHELLS

DIFFICULTY:
HARD

You can use manicotti pasta instead of large shells. You will need to use a small spoon to stuff the cheese mixture inside the cooked manicotti.

SERVES 8

1 (12-ounce) package jumbo pasta shells

3 cups pasta sauce, divided into 1-cup and 2-cup portions

2 large eggs

1 (15-ounce) container ricotta cheese

2 cups chopped broccoli

1 tablespoon chopped fresh parsley

¼ teaspoon salt

¼ teaspoon ground black pepper

¾ cup grated Parmesan cheese

2 cups shredded mozzarella cheese, divided into 2 (1-cup) portions

1. Preheat the oven to 350°F.

2. Pour water into a large pot until it is two-thirds full. Place the pot over high heat and bring the water to a boil. Add the pasta shells and cook for 8 minutes. Place a colander in the sink and ask an adult to help you carefully pour the pasta and water into the colander to drain.

3. Spread 1 cup of the sauce into the bottom of a 9-by-13-inch baking pan.

4. In a large bowl, mix the eggs, ricotta, broccoli, parsley, salt, pepper, Parmesan, and 1 cup of mozzarella.

5. Take a shell and stuff it with the cheese mixture, then lay the shell in the baking pan on top of the sauce. Repeat with the remaining shells.

6. Pour the remaining 2 cups of the sauce over the shells. Top with the remaining 1 cup of the mozzarella cheese.

7. Bake for 25–30 minutes until the cheese is lightly browned. Use pot holders to remove the pan from the oven. Cool for 10 minutes before serving.

PER SERVING

Calories: 440 | Fat: 19g | Sodium: 850mg | Carbohydrates: 46g | Fiber: 1g | Sugar: 11g | Protein: 27g

CORN, TOMATO, AND AVOCADO SALAD

This colorful salad is bursting with fresh flavors. It's good to serve on the side when you're having grilled chicken for dinner.

SERVES 4

1 (10-ounce) bag frozen corn kernels

1 medium avocado

½ pint cherry tomatoes, cut in half

4 ounces small fresh mozzarella balls

½ teaspoon dried cilantro

½ teaspoon salt

¼ teaspoon ground black pepper

1 tablespoon olive oil

1½ teaspoons lime juice

1. Put the corn in a colander. Run warm water over the corn until it thaws. Let all the water drain out, then put the corn in a large bowl.

2. Carefully cut the avocado in half. Discard the pit and remove the peel. Chop the avocado into large chunks (ask an adult for help).

3. Add the avocado, cherry tomatoes, and mozzarella cheese to the bowl with the corn. Sprinkle with the cilantro, salt, and pepper. Mix carefully with a wooden spoon.

4. Mix the oil and lime juice in a small bowl with a whisk. Drizzle the mixture over the salad and serve it right away.

PER SERVING

Calories: 250 | Fat: 18g | Sodium: 360mg | Carbohydrates: 15g | Fiber: 4g | Sugar: 5g | Protein: 9g

Fun Fact

Small balls of fresh mozzarella cheese are called "bocconcini." The name comes from the Italian word for "mouth," because they are bite-sized.

Chapter 7

DESSERTS AND SPECIAL TREATS

Desserts are fun to make, delicious to eat, and rewarding to share with others. Every once in a while, we all deserve a treat, right? Make some today for the special people in your life, like your grandparents, teachers, or friends. You'll be so proud of yourself!

DIFFICULTY:
MEDIUM

DOUBLE CHOCOLATE CHIP COOKIES

These cookies are great when you have a craving for something super chocolatey. Bake them for 8 minutes for chewy cookies and 10 minutes for crispier ones.

MAKES 30 COOKIES

½ cup granulated sugar

½ cup light brown sugar

½ cup (1 stick) butter, softened

2 large eggs

½ teaspoon vanilla extract

1¾ cups all-purpose flour

¼ cup unsweetened cocoa powder

1 teaspoon baking soda

¼ teaspoon salt

1 cup semisweet chocolate chips

1. Preheat the oven to 375°F.
2. In a large mixing bowl, use an electric mixer to combine the granulated sugar, brown sugar, butter, eggs, and vanilla. Mix until smooth.
3. Add the flour, cocoa powder, baking soda, and salt. Mix again until the batter is smooth and creamy. Use a wooden spoon to stir in the chocolate chips.
4. Use a tablespoon or cookie scoop to form small balls of dough. Put the balls of dough on two large ungreased baking sheets. You should be able to fit fifteen cookies on each sheet. Make sure they are not too close together. They will need about 1 inch on each side to spread out.
5. Bake one sheet at a time for 8–10 minutes, until the cookies are light golden brown.
6. Use pot holders to remove the baking sheet from the oven. Let the cookies cool for 1 minute on the pan, then move the cookies to a cooling rack using a spatula. Cool 5 minutes more before serving.

PER SERVING (2 COOKIES)

Calories: 240 | Fat: 11g | Sodium: 135mg | Carbohydrates: 35g | Fiber: 1g | Sugar: 23g | Protein: 4g

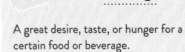

craving:

A great desire, taste, or hunger for a certain food or beverage.

GRAHAM ICE CREAM SANDWICHES

These sandwiches can be made with any flavor of ice cream, sherbet, or frozen yogurt. Dip the edges of the sandwich in candy sprinkles, mini chips, or nuts for an extra-fun snack.

SERVES 2

2 large graham crackers, each broken into two squares

½ cup vanilla ice cream, slightly softened

1. Place two of the graham cracker squares on a flat surface. Scoop ¼ cup of the ice cream and place it on one square, then place the rest of the ice cream on the second square.

2. Top the sandwiches with the remaining two graham cracker squares.

3. Serve the ice cream sandwiches right away or wrap them in plastic wrap and put them in the freezer to serve them later.

PER SERVING

Calories: 90 | Fat: 4g | Sodium: 40mg | Carbohydrates: 11g | Fiber: 0g | Sugar: 8g | Protein: 1g

Cut the Cake

How would you cut a round cake into nine pieces with only four cuts of the knife?

BANANA SPLIT ICE CREAM PIE

What's better than ice cream after a cookout? To turn dessert into a sundae party, set out the fudge sauce, whipped cream, cherries, and nuts so each person can top their own slice of pie.

SERVES 8

2 large bananas, peeled

1 (9-ounce) ready-to-use graham cracker piecrust

1 quart vanilla ice cream, softened

½ cup hot fudge sauce

2 cups nondairy frozen whipped topping, thawed

8 maraschino cherries

1 cup chopped walnuts

1. Slice the bananas and lay them out in the bottom of the piecrust.
2. Scoop out the softened ice cream and spread it evenly over the bananas with a spatula.
3. Cover the pie with plastic wrap and freeze it for at least 2 hours to harden the ice cream.
4. Remove the pie from the freezer, unwrap it, and let it soften for 5 minutes.
5. Spread the hot fudge sauce over the ice cream, then spoon the whipped topping on top. Decorate the pie with the cherries and walnuts.
6. Let the pie soften for about 5 minutes before you cut it. Wrap leftovers in plastic wrap and keep them in the freezer.

PER SERVING

Calories: 460 | Fat: 27g | Sodium: 210mg | Carbohydrates: 48g | Fiber: 1g | Sugar: 32g | Protein: 7g

Everybody Loves...

Can you guess which flavor of ice cream is the most popular in the United States? It's not chocolate, strawberry, cookies and cream, or rocky road—it's plain old vanilla!

DIFFICULTY: MEDIUM

THUMBPRINT SURPRISES

Try different flavors of fruit preserves to make these cookies more colorful.

MAKES 48 COOKIES

½ cup granulated sugar

1 cup (2 sticks) butter, softened

½ cup light brown sugar

1 large egg

1 teaspoon vanilla extract

3 cups all-purpose flour

½ teaspoon salt

½ cup strawberry jam

1. Preheat the oven to 350°F.

2. Put the granulated sugar on a small plate or in a bowl and set it aside.

3. In a large mixing bowl, use an electric mixer to beat the butter and brown sugar until smooth. Add the egg and vanilla and beat again. Gradually beat in the flour and salt.

4. Scoop up about 1 tablespoon of dough and roll it into a ball, about 1 inch in size.

5. Roll the dough in the granulated sugar to coat the outside of the ball. Put the balls onto ungreased baking sheets, leaving about 2 inches between each cookie.

6. Slightly press down on the ball with your thumb to form a well in the middle.

7. Spoon about ½ teaspoon of the jam into each well.

8. Bake 1 baking sheet at a time for 10–12 minutes until the cookies are lightly browned.

9. Remove the baking sheet from the oven using pot holders. Let the cookies cool for 1 minute on the baking sheet, then move the cookies to a cooling rack using a spatula. Cool 15 minutes more before serving.

PER SERVING (2 COOKIES)

Calories: 170 | Fat: 8g | Sodium: 55mg | Carbohydrates: 24g | Fiber: 0g | Sugar: 13g | Protein: 2g

FAVORITE FUDGE

For a rocky road fudge, add chopped nuts and mini marshmallows to the fudge before refrigerating.

MAKES 24 PIECES

3 cups sugar

¾ cup (1½ sticks) butter

⅔ cup evaporated milk

1 (12-ounce) package semisweet chocolate chips

1 (7-ounce) jar marshmallow creme

1 teaspoon vanilla extract

1. Spray a 9-by-13-inch pan with nonstick cooking spray.
2. In a large saucepan, combine the sugar, butter, and evaporated milk over medium-high heat.
3. Stirring constantly with a wooden spoon, heat the mixture until it boils, about 5 minutes.
4. Turn off the heat and remove the pan from the burner.
5. Add the chocolate chips, stirring until they melt. Add the marshmallow creme and vanilla and stir until the mixture is well blended.
6. Pour the mixture into the prepared pan.
7. Refrigerate until the fudge hardens (at least 4 hours) before cutting.

PER SERVING (1 PIECE)

Calories: 240 | Fat: 10g | Sodium: 15mg | Carbohydrates: 41g | Fiber: 0g | Sugar: 37g | Protein: 1g

A Happy Mistake

Fudge is a word that people used to use when something was messed up. Some people say that the first fudge was made when someone's batch of caramels was "fudged" up.

ULTIMATE PEANUT BUTTER CHOCOLATE SQUARES

DIFFICULTY:
MEDIUM

You can't go wrong with these peanut butter and chocolate treats. Not only are they easy to make, but they are also a hit at every party.

MAKES 48 SQUARES

¾ cup graham cracker crumbs

1 cup smooth peanut butter

1 cup (2 sticks) butter, melted

3½ cups powdered sugar

1½ cups semisweet chocolate chips

1. Spray a 9-by-13-inch pan with nonstick cooking spray. Set aside.
2. In a large bowl, combine the graham cracker crumbs, peanut butter, melted butter, and powdered sugar. Mix well with a wooden spoon.
3. Spread the batter out into the prepared pan.
4. Put the chocolate chips in a microwave-safe bowl and place the bowl in the microwave. Heat the chocolate chips for 30 seconds on high. Remove the bowl from the microwave and stir the chocolate. Return the bowl to the microwave and turn it on high for another 15 seconds. Remove the bowl and stir it again. Most of the chocolate chips should be melted. If not, microwave for another 10 seconds. It's okay if a few of the chips are not melted; they will melt into the hot chocolate as you stir.
5. Use a spatula to spread the melted chocolate over the peanut butter mixture in the pan.
6. Place the pan in the refrigerator to cool for at least 2 hours before cutting into squares.

PER SERVING (1 SQUARE)

Calories: 140 | Fat: 9g | Sodium: 35mg | Carbohydrates: 16g | Fiber: 0g | Sugar: 13g | Protein: 2g

DIFFICULTY:
MEDIUM

WORLD'S BEST BROWNIES

You will receive lots of compliments for these brownies because everyone loves them. They make a wonderful treat to share.

MAKES 16 BROWNIES

1 cup all-purpose flour

1½ cups granulated sugar

¾ cup unsweetened cocoa

½ cup light brown sugar

½ teaspoon salt

½ cup (1 stick) butter

3 large eggs

½ teaspoon vanilla extract

¼ cup semisweet chocolate chips

¼ cup white chocolate chips

½ cup chopped walnuts

1. Preheat the oven to 350°F. Spray a 9-inch square pan with nonstick cooking spray.
2. In a large bowl, use a wooden spoon to combine the flour, sugar, cocoa, brown sugar, and salt.
3. Melt the butter in a small saucepan over low heat. Add the melted butter, eggs, and vanilla to the sugar mixture. Mix well.
4. Stir in the chocolate chips, white chocolate chips, and nuts.
5. Pour the batter into the prepared pan.
6. Bake for 30–35 minutes, or until done. Remove the pan from the oven using pot holders and put it on a cooling rack. Let the brownies cool for at least 1 hour before cutting and serving.

PER SERVING (1 BROWNIE)

Calories: 250 | Fat: 11g | Sodium: 90mg | Carbohydrates: 38g | Fiber: 2g | Sugar: 29g | Protein: 4g

Is It Done Yet?

To test for doneness, insert a toothpick into the center of the brownies. If the toothpick comes out clean, the brownies are done. If there is batter on the toothpick, the brownies need to cook another 1–2 minutes. Then test again with a clean toothpick.

CHOCOLATE PEANUT BUTTER PUDDING

DIFFICULTY:
EASY

Try substituting chunky peanut butter for a crunchier taste. Top the pudding with whipped topping and chopped peanuts if you like.

SERVES 4

2 cups cold milk

1 (3.9-ounce) package instant chocolate pudding mix

½ cup smooth peanut butter

1. Pour the milk into a medium bowl. Add the pudding mix and beat with a whisk for 2 minutes. Use the whisk to stir in the peanut butter.
2. Pour the pudding into four small dishes.
3. Put the bowls in the refrigerator for at least 30 minutes before serving.

PER SERVING

Calories: 370 | Fat: 20g | Sodium: 630mg | Carbohydrates: 37g | Fiber: 2g | Sugar: 27g | Protein: 11g

Jimmy likes...

...broccoli, *but not bok choy*

...cabbage, *but not celery*

...scallions, *but not spinach*

...zucchini, *but not squash*

...lettuce, *but not lima beans*

...peppers, *but not parsley*

Can you figure out the secret to which vegetables Jimmy likes?

DIFFICULTY:
MEDIUM

FRUIT AND COOKIE PIZZA

When you place the fruit on the pizza, you can decorate it any way you want. You could spell a name, make a flag for a holiday, or even create colorful patterns, like a rainbow.

SERVES 12

1 (16.5-ounce) package refrigerated sugar cookie dough

1 (8-ounce) package cream cheese, softened

¼ cup sugar

1 teaspoon vanilla extract

1 small banana, peeled and sliced

1 small kiwifruit, peeled and sliced

1 cup sliced strawberries

½ cup blueberries

¼ cup apple jelly

2 teaspoons water

1. Preheat the oven to 350°F.

2. Spread the entire roll of cookie dough out onto a large ungreased baking sheet or pizza pan. Bake 12–14 minutes, or until lightly browned. Use pot holders to remove the pan from the oven. Place the pan on a cooling rack and cool the crust completely, about 30 minutes.

3. Put the cream cheese, sugar, and vanilla in a large bowl and mix well with a wooden spoon. Use a spatula to spread the mixture over the top of the cooled crust.

4. Place the fruit on top of the cream cheese layer.

5. In a small microwave-safe bowl, combine the jelly and water. Heat the mixture in the microwave for 20–30 seconds on high until it is melted and spreadable. Brush the glaze over the fruit on the pizza.

6. Refrigerate the pizza for at least 2 hours before serving. Cut it into pieces with a pizza cutter.

PER SERVING

Calories: 280 | Fat: 13g | Sodium: 200mg | Carbohydrates: 39g | Fiber: 1g | Sugar: 26g | Protein: 3g

FRUITY NACHOS

Who says nachos have to be made with cheese, meat, and vegetables?
These sweet nachos would make a great dessert or party snack.

SERVES 6

6 (6-inch) flour tortillas

2 tablespoons butter

⅓ cup sugar

¾ teaspoon ground cinnamon

2 tablespoons chocolate syrup

2 tablespoons caramel sauce

½ cup sliced strawberries

¼ cup raspberries

¼ cup blueberries or blackberries

1. Preheat the oven to 400°F. Line two baking sheets with parchment paper.
2. Use a pizza cutter to cut the tortillas into six wedges each. Put the wedges in a large zip-top plastic bag.
3. Put the butter in a small microwave-safe bowl and microwave it for 15–20 seconds until the butter is melted. Pour the butter over the tortilla wedges in the bag.
4. Mix the sugar and cinnamon in a small bowl with a wooden spoon. Pour the mixture into the bag. Seal the bag and shake it up until the wedges are coated.
5. Place the wedges on the baking sheets in a single layer. Bake for 6–8 minutes until the chips are browned and crunchy around the edges.
6. Remove the baking sheets from the oven using pot holders. Let the chips cool for 15 minutes.
7. Place the chips on a large plate. Drizzle them with the chocolate syrup and caramel sauce.
8. Top the nachos with the berries. Serve right away.

PER SERVING

Calories: 220 | Fat: 7g | Sodium: 300mg |
Carbohydrates: 37g | Fiber: 1g | Sugar: 19g |
Protein: 3g

Thanks, Nacho!

Nachos got their name from a waiter who made a batch for a group of hungry Americans at a restaurant in Mexico. His nickname was Nacho, so he named his creation after himself.

FRESH FRUIT AND YOGURT PARFAIT

Kids and adults alike will enjoy this fruit parfait. Try various types of fresh fruit and different flavors of yogurt to please everyone. It's great for a quick, healthy breakfast, a snack, or a sweet ending to a meal.

SERVES 1

1 (6-ounce) container low-fat vanilla yogurt

¼ cup fresh raspberries

¼ cup fresh blueberries

¼ cup fresh blackberries

2 tablespoons granola

1. Start with a parfait glass, a tall (8-ounce) drinking glass, or a glass bowl. Spoon ¼ cup of the yogurt into the bottom of the glass.

2. Add a layer of berries and top with more yogurt. Repeat the layers until all of the ingredients are used up.

3. Top the parfait with the granola. Eat immediately.

PER SERVING

Calories: 250 | Fat: 3.5g | Sodium: 105mg | Carbohydrates: 47g | Fiber: 5g | Sugar: 35g | Protein: 10g

Kitchen Tip

Get all ingredients out before you start to cook so you don't have to hunt down any ingredients while you are in the middle of a recipe.

You Scream, I Scream

Can you ever have too much ice cream?
Maybe...see how you feel after you have
eaten your way from START to END!

Start

End

Chapter 8

SMOOTHIES AND BEVERAGES

If you have never made a smoothie or fun beverage at home, now is the time to try it. You will need a blender for some of these drinks, and tall glasses for all of them. But those are the only rules! You can use fruit, yogurt, ice cream, milk, juice...anything that sounds like it might taste good. Once you learn how to make a few of these drinks, you'll be able to make lots of different kinds to match your taste—or your mood!

CREAMY SHAKE

You'll go nuts over this Creamy Shake. You can freeze it for an extra-delightful treat.

SERVES 1

1 cup vanilla ice cream   ½ cup orange juice

1. Combine the ice cream and the orange juice in a blender. Put the lid on and blend for 1 minute, or until smooth.
2. Pour into a tall glass and drink right away.

PER SERVING

Calories: 330 | Fat: 15g | Sodium: 105mg | Carbohydrates: 44g | Fiber: 0g | Sugar: 38g | Protein: 5g

TROPICAL SMOOTHIE

For added decoration, garnish the glasses with a slice or two of fresh fruit or a mini paper umbrella. It's almost like you're on vacation!

SERVES 2

1 cup orange juice

1 medium banana, peeled and sliced

½ cup frozen mango or peach slices

½ cup frozen sliced strawberries

1. Put all of the ingredients in a blender. Put the lid on and blend for 1 minute, or until smooth.
2. Pour into two tall glasses and serve right away.

PER SERVING

Calories: 150 | Fat: .5g | Sodium: 0mg | Carbohydrates: 36g | Fiber: 3g | Sugar: 25g | Protein: 2g

BEST BANANA-BERRY SMOOTHIE

You can enjoy this smoothie any time of year. It's delicious, refreshing, and good for you. And it's a great choice for breakfast on the go!

DIFFICULTY: EASY

Drink Up!

Can you find the twelve beverages hiding in the glass?

CIDER
FLOAT
HOT COCOA
ICED TEA
JUICE
FIZZ
LEMONADE
MILK
PUNCH

SHAKE
SMOOTHIE
SODA

```
I C E D T E A P J H O
F I Z H O A T O U F H
P S E T K D S O I I O
R M D F L O A T O Z T
E O A J L S U H T Z C
D O N U Z S O S D M O
I T O S M O O H T O C
C H M I I P U A P E O
Q I E B L J U K U S A
  E L X K I E E N O
  E J U I C E T K D
    P U H C N U P
      E N S
```

SERVES 2

1 medium banana, peeled, sliced, and frozen

¼ cup frozen blueberries

¼ cup frozen raspberries

¼ cup frozen sliced strawberries

1 (5.3-ounce) container low-fat vanilla Greek yogurt

¾ cup milk

1. Put all of the ingredients in a blender. Put the lid on and blend for 1 minute, or until smooth.
2. Pour into two tall glasses and serve right away.

PER SERVING

Calories: 190 | Fat: 3.5g | Sodium: 70mg | Carbohydrates: 32g | Fiber: 4g | Sugar: 21g | Protein: 10g

JUST PEACHY SMOOTHIE

This drink is best in the summer, when the freshest fruit is available.

DIFFICULTY:
EASY

SERVES 2

2 cups vanilla ice cream

½ cup milk

1 medium fresh peach, peeled, pitted, and cut up into chunks

1 tablespoon honey

(1) Put all of the ingredients in a blender. Put the lid on and blend for 1 minute, or until smooth.

(2) Pour into two tall glasses and serve right away.

PER SERVING

Calories: 370 | Fat: 17g | Sodium: 130mg | Carbohydrates: 50g | Fiber: 1g | Sugar: 45g | Protein: 7g

* * * * * * **Seeing Stars** * * * * * *

**All the vowels in this puzzle have been replaced.
Oh my stars, can you still read the riddle?**

WHY D*DN'T TH* *R*NGE
CR*SS TH* R**D?

*T R*N **T *F J**C*!

**DIFFICULTY:
EASY**

GRAPE ICE DELIGHT

Use fun-colored straws and iced tea spoons to get every last drop!

SERVES 1

½ cup lemon or lime sherbet

½ cup grape juice

½ cup ginger ale

1. Put the sherbet in a tall glass.
2. Pour the grape juice over the sherbet and then slowly pour the ginger ale over the top.
3. Serve right away.

PER SERVING

Calories: 260 | Fat: 2g | Sodium: 65mg | Carbohydrates: 60g | Fiber: 0g | Sugar: 53g | Protein: 2g

**DIFFICULTY:
MEDIUM**

HOT APPLE CIDER

Hot cider is a wonderful drink to serve at a party or to sip on a cool fall night.

SERVES 8

8 cups apple cider

1 medium unpeeled orange, cut into thin slices

2 cinnamon sticks

6 whole cloves

1. In a large saucepan, stir all the ingredients with a wooden spoon.
2. Heat over medium-high heat just to boiling.
3. Reduce the heat to low and simmer, uncovered, for 30 minutes. Use a slotted spoon to remove the orange slices, cinnamon sticks, and cloves before serving. Ladle the cider into mugs and serve hot.

PER SERVING

Calories: 130 | Fat: 0g | Sodium: 25mg | Carbohydrates: 32g | Fiber: 1g | Sugar: 28g | Protein: 0g

TANGY ORANGE FIZZ

DIFFICULTY:
EASY

If you make a double batch of this fun drink for a party, pour the Tangy Orange Fizz into a punch bowl with ice on the side so the punch doesn't get watery.

SERVES 6

2 cups lemonade

2 cups orange juice

2 cups sparkling water or seltzer

2 cups ice cubes

1. In a large pitcher, combine all of the ingredients.
2. Stir well with a wooden spoon. Serve right away.

PER SERVING

Calories: 70 | Fat: 0g | Sodium: 25mg | Carbohydrates: 18g | Fiber: 0g | Sugar: 16g | Protein: 1g

PURPLE COW

DIFFICULTY:
EASY

You will love this great taste combination. There's nothing better!

SERVES 1

¼ cup grape soda

½ cup vanilla ice cream

½ teaspoon vanilla extract

3 ice cubes

1. Combine all of the ingredients in a blender. Put the lid on and blend for 1 minute, or until smooth.
2. Pour into a tall glass and serve right away.

PER SERVING

Calories: 170 | Fat: 7g | Sodium: 65mg | Carbohydrates: 23g | Fiber: 0g | Sugar: 21g | Protein: 2g

carbonation:

Occurs when carbon dioxide is dissolved in water, resulting in the "fizz" found in seltzer and soda.

CREAMY DREAMY ROOT BEER FLOAT

Watch the foam appear as you pour the root beer. What a treat!

SERVES 1

½ cup vanilla ice cream

1 cup root beer

1. Put the ice cream in a tall glass. Slowly pour the root beer over the top.
2. Serve right away.

PER SERVING

Calories: 250 | Fat: 7g | Sodium: 105mg | Carbohydrates: 47g | Fiber: 0g | Sugar: 44g | Protein: 2g

I'm Thirsty

These kids are all thirsty, but everyone wants to drink something different. Crack the code on each glass to figure out who is sipping what. Remember—there's a different code on each glass!

13-9-12-11

epos

H2O

KVJDF

Where Did Root Beer First Come From?

Many believe that root beer was first made by accident by a pharmacist trying to create a miracle drug with roots, berries, and herbs.

CHOCO-BANANA-AVOCADO SMOOTHIE

It's a snack, a beverage, or a healthy treat—this yummy smoothie gives you the best of all worlds!

SERVES 2

½ cup milk

¼ cup low-fat vanilla Greek yogurt

½ medium avocado, peeled and pitted (ask an adult to help)

1 small banana, peeled, sliced, and frozen

1 tablespoon unsweetened cocoa

1 teaspoon sugar

1 Combine all of the ingredients in a blender. Put the lid on and blend for 1 minute, or until smooth.

2 Pour into two glasses and serve right away.

PER SERVING

Calories: 210 | Fat: 11g | Sodium: 45mg | Carbohydrates: 25g | Fiber: 6g | Sugar: 15g | Protein: 7g

Freezing a Banana

When a banana becomes too ripe and soft to eat, you can freeze it to keep on hand for smoothies and frozen beverages. Peel the banana and then wrap it in plastic wrap and place it in the freezer; otherwise, you will have a hard time removing the peel.

Chapter 9

PARTY TIME

We all love special holidays, family gatherings, and parties. Foods are an important part of each of them. Here are a few special-occasion recipes you may enjoy trying. Start a collection of your own favorites too.

DIFFICULTY:
EASY

PARTY-TIME PUNCH

You can jazz up your punch by adding scoops of orange, lemon, or lime sherbet.

SERVES 12

1 (12-ounce) can frozen orange juice concentrate, thawed

1 (12-ounce) can frozen lemonade concentrate, thawed

1 (2-liter) bottle ginger ale

2 medium unpeeled oranges, cut into thin slices

3 cups ice cubes

1. Combine the orange juice concentrate, lemonade concentrate, and ginger ale in a large punch bowl. Mix well with a wooden spoon.
2. Add the orange slices to the punch and stir in the ice.
3. Serve right away.

PER SERVING

Calories: 170 | Fat: 0g | Sodium: 25mg | Carbohydrates: 43g | Fiber: 1g | Sugar: 39g | Protein: 1g

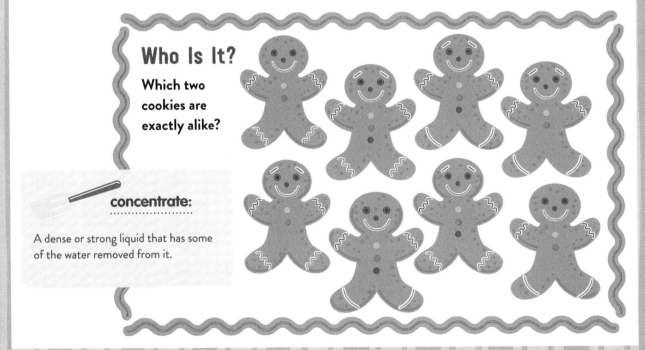

Who Is It?

Which two cookies are exactly alike?

concentrate:

A dense or strong liquid that has some of the water removed from it.

VALENTINE PIZZA

DIFFICULTY: **MEDIUM**

You can decorate your heart-shaped pizza with any toppings you like. The options are endless.

SERVES 6

1 (14-ounce) pre-baked Italian pizza crust

¾ cup pizza sauce

1 (8-ounce) package shredded mozzarella cheese

1 cup chopped red bell pepper

8 ounces sliced mushrooms

2 ounces sliced pepperoni

1. Preheat the oven to 425°F.
2. Using kitchen shears, cut a wedge out of the round pizza crust to create a heart shape. Place the crust on a baking sheet or pizza pan.
3. Spread the pizza sauce over the top of the crust with a wooden spoon. Sprinkle the cheese over the sauce.
4. Top the pizza with the bell peppers, mushrooms, and pepperoni.
5. Place the pizza in the oven and bake for 8–10 minutes, or until the cheese is melted and slightly browned. Use pot holders to remove the pizza from the oven.
6. Let the pizza cool for 5 minutes, then use a pizza cutter to cut the pizza into six slices. Serve hot.

PER SERVING

Calories: 390 | Fat: 16g | Sodium: 900mg | Carbohydrates: 41g | Fiber: 1g | Sugar: 7g | Protein: 20g

Fun Fact

The largest pizza on record in the world was 131 feet in diameter. Named Ottavia after Rome's first emperor, the pizza was created in Italy by Dovilio Nardi. It was made gluten-free to help bring awareness to celiac disease; people with this disease can't eat wheat and other common foods that contain gluten.

FOURTH OF JULY CAKE

You will love decorating this cake for this special holiday. The entire family can help. If you like, you can use strawberry slices instead of raspberries.

DIFFICULTY: MEDIUM

SERVES 12

1 (15.25-ounce) box classic yellow cake mix

1 cup water

⅓ cup vegetable oil

3 large eggs

1 (16-ounce) container prepared white frosting

1 pint fresh blueberries

2 pints fresh raspberries

1. Preheat the oven to 350°F. Spray a 9-by-13-inch baking pan with nonstick cooking spray.

2. In a large bowl, blend the cake mix, water, oil, and eggs using an electric mixer. Beat until smooth, about 2 minutes.

3. Scrape the batter into the prepared pan using a spatula. Place the pan in the oven and bake for 23–28 minutes, or until a toothpick stuck into the middle of the cake comes out clean.

4. Use pot holders to remove the pan from the oven. Place the pan on a cooling rack and cool for at least 1 hour. Spread the frosting over the cooled cake in the pan.

5. Place fifty blueberries in the upper-left corner—for the fifty stars on a flag. Place the raspberries in rows to make stripes on a flag.

6. Serve right away or refrigerate until you're ready to serve it.

Fun Fact

Each raspberry is made of about one hundred tiny fruits called "drupelets," and each of them has its own tiny seed inside. Raspberries can be either red, black, purple, or yellow. The yellow ones are the sweetest.

PER SERVING

Calories: 400 | Fat: 15g | Sodium: 360mg | Carbohydrates: 64g | Fiber: 2g | Sugar: 43g | Protein: 3g

MINI PARTY CHEESE BALLS

These little bites make a fun party treat. Put them on a platter with crackers and fresh vegetables, like baby carrots, bell pepper slices, or celery sticks.

SERVES 6

4 ounces cream cheese, softened

¼ cup canned crushed pineapple, drained

1 tablespoon finely chopped red bell pepper

1 tablespoon finely chopped scallions

¼ teaspoon salt

¼ teaspoon ground black pepper

½ cup finely chopped almonds

6 whole roasted almonds

1. Put the cream cheese, pineapple, bell pepper, scallions, salt, and black pepper in a medium bowl. Use a wooden spoon to mix it all together.

2. Divide the mixture into six equal portions and roll each into a ball, about 1½ inches wide.

3. Put the chopped almonds in a medium bowl. Roll the cheese balls in the almonds to cover the outside of each ball. Press a whole almond into the top of each ball.

4. Place the balls on a plate, cover with plastic wrap, and refrigerate for at least 1 hour.

5. Take the balls out of the refrigerator and remove the plastic wrap before serving.

PER SERVING

Calories: 140 | Fat: 12g | Sodium: 170mg | Carbohydrates: 6g | Fiber: 2g | Sugar: 2g | Protein: 4g

Decorate a Cheese Tree

For a holiday party appetizer, you can form each ball into a mini holiday tree and decorate them with tiny bits of chopped vegetables or fruits.

CELEBRATION ICE CREAM PIE

DIFFICULTY: **EASY**

Who doesn't love ice cream pies? This recipe is so easy that you can make it over and over again with your favorite ice cream flavors.

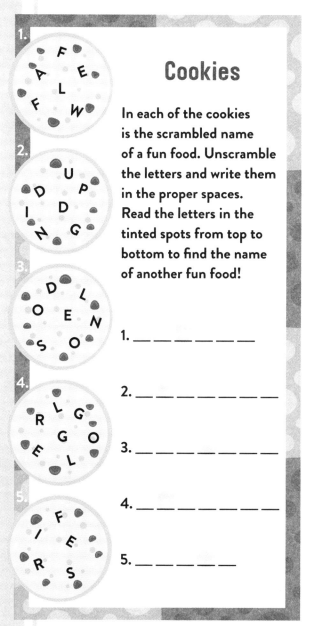

Cookies

In each of the cookies is the scrambled name of a fun food. Unscramble the letters and write them in the proper spaces. Read the letters in the tinted spots from top to bottom to find the name of another fun food!

1. _ _ _ _ _ _ _

2. _ _ _ _ _ _ _

3. _ _ _ _ _ _ _

4. _ _ _ _ _ _ _

5. _ _ _ _ _ _

SERVES 8

2 quarts chocolate chip ice cream, softened

1 (9-inch) prepared chocolate piecrust

½ cup sliced strawberries

2 tablespoons chocolate syrup

1. Spoon the softened ice cream into the piecrust and spread it out evenly with a spatula.

2. Decorate the top of the pie with the strawberries. Drizzle the syrup over the strawberries.

3. Freeze the pie for at least 1 hour before serving.

PER SERVING

Calories: 410 | Fat: 15g | Sodium: 190mg | Carbohydrates: 62g | Fiber: 0g | Sugar: 39g | Protein: 6g

HALLOWEEN SPIDER BITES

You can use gummy spiders, gummy bats, gummy worms, or any other critters you choose on your webs.

MAKES 8 COOKIES

8 flat chocolate wafer cookies

1 (0.67-ounce) tube white decorating gel

8 gummy candy spiders

1. Place the cookies on a large flat plate.
2. Using the decorating gel, draw three circles on each cookie, one large one around the outside rim, a smaller one on the inside, and an even smaller one in the middle.
3. Using a toothpick, start at the inside middle of a cookie and run the toothpick all the way to the outside edge. Do this about four times around the cookie. This will create a "web." Repeat with the remaining cookies.
4. Place a gummy spider on top of each cookie.

PER SERVING (2 COOKIES)

Calories: 117 | Fat: 2.5g | Sodium: 107mg | Carbohydrates: 22g | Fiber: 0g | Sugar: 10g | Protein: 1g

Make Your Own Spiders

You can make your own gummy spiders from gumdrops and thin licorice strings. Cut the licorice strings into eight small strips (legs) and insert them into the gumdrop.

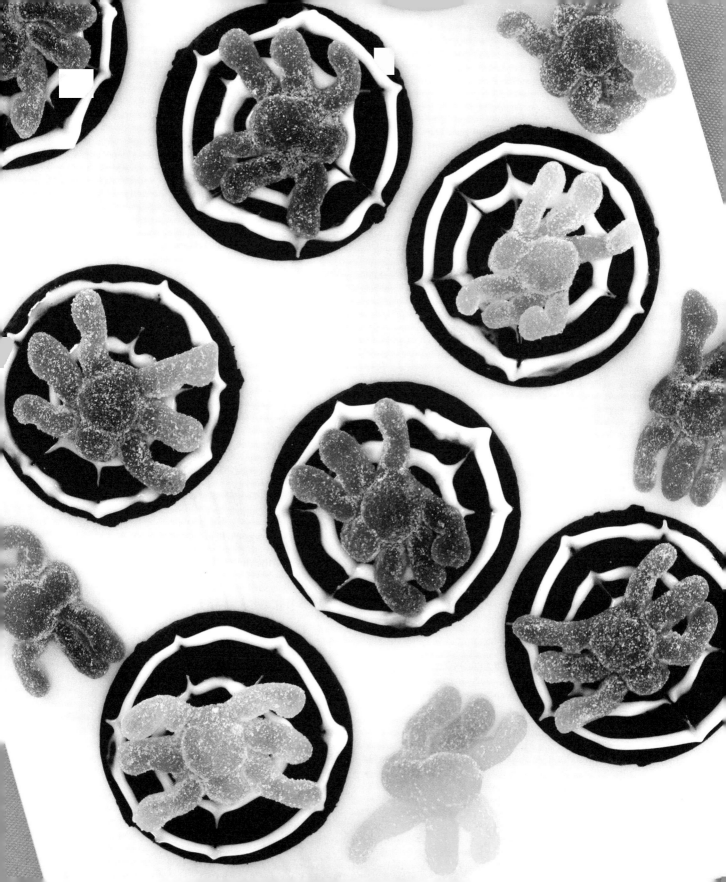

In the Kitchen

Use the clues below to fill in the puzzle grid on the facing page. Be careful—some of the answers are silly, not serious! We left you some T-I-D-B-I-T-S to help you get started.

ACROSS

1 In the middle of the day you eat _____.

3 All the recipes in this book make things that taste ____!

5 A short name for a long sandwich

7 A crunchy shell filled with meat, vegetables, and cheese

10 Do this to potatoes to make them smooth and fluffy.

11 It sounds like you need to be a member to eat this sandwich.

13 To cut a thin piece

14 Pot topper

15 You'll use one of these to flip a pancake.

17 Always do this before you start cooking.

21 Cut a carrot into tiny cubes.

22 It would be great to have one of these to clean the kitchen!

26 Used to wrap burritos

30 Put something in the microwave and "___" it.

31 Yeast helps bread to ____.

32 Sweet and crunchy oats, seeds, and nuts that are good for breakfast or for snacks

33 Why was the ice cream lonely? Because the banana ____!

DOWN

1 You can use this in a salad.

2 Tortilla chips with melted cheese on top

4 Treats baked 12 at a time in metal cups

6 Tiny vegetables are called "___."

8 A round and chewy breakfast bread

9 Creamy soup that's made with corn or clams

11 A bowl with holes for liquid to drain out

12 What you find at the center of a cherry

16 The opposite of "rightunders"

17 You beat eggs or cream with this.

18 What does a gingerbread man put on his bed? Cookie ____!

19 What makes bread rise?

20 On a hot day, it's good to drink cold lemon___.

23 A thin stream of liquid (or a light rain!)

24 This kind of Italian "pie" is a lunch or dinner favorite.

25 Use a spatula to ____ your pancakes.

27 Waffle topper

28 Who likes "woofles" for breakfast? The ___!

29 A good thing to fill with ice cream

WHITE HOT CHOCOLATE

We're all familiar with hot chocolate, but have you ever made this famous drink with white chocolate? Top mugs of White Hot Chocolate with red sprinkles, mini marshmallows, crushed peppermint candies, or cinnamon candies for a festive holiday look.

SERVES 2

2 cups milk

⅓ cup white chocolate chips

½ teaspoon vanilla extract

1. Combine the milk, chocolate chips, and vanilla in a medium saucepan. Heat over medium heat.
2. Stir with a wooden spoon just until the chips are melted. (Don't let the mixture boil.)
3. Pour the mixture into two mugs and serve right away.

PER SERVING

Calories: 340 | Fat: 18g | Sodium: 130mg | Carbohydrates: 36g | Fiber: 0g | Sugar: 36g | Protein: 10g

The silly answer is, "It was a total flop!"

What's the silly question? To find out, use the rules to cross words out of the grid. Read the remaining words from left to right and top to bottom.

Cross out...

...fruits that are red

...three-letter words that contain "E"

...words that rhyme with FLOP

APPLE	DROP	HOW	EAT
CHOP	DID	POMEGRANATE	SHOP
BET	POP	CHERRY	YOUR
PINEAPPLE	HEN	CROP	STRAWBERRY
MOP	UPSIDE DOWN	TOE	CAKE
HOP	STOP	TURN	TOP
OUT	HEW	RASPBERRY	WET

WINTER WREATHS

You can substitute colored sugars for the granola for a different, more colorful look.

DIFFICULTY:
MEDIUM

SERVES 8

1 (8-ounce) can refrigerated crescent roll dough

2 tablespoons milk

1 drop green food coloring

2 tablespoons sugar

½ teaspoon ground cinnamon

½ cup granola, crushed into small pieces

8 maraschino cherries

1. Preheat the oven to 375°F.
2. Open the crescent rolls and separate them into eight pieces. Roll each piece into a log, about 6–8 inches long. Connect the two ends to make a circle. Place the circles on a large baking sheet lined with parchment paper.
3. Mix the milk and food coloring in a small bowl. Using a clean pastry brush or paint brush, brush the mixture on top of the dough wreaths.
4. Combine the sugar and cinnamon in a small bowl or shaker bottle. Sprinkle each wreath with the cinnamon-sugar mixture. Sprinkle the granola on top of the cinnamon-sugar mixture.
5. Place the pan in the oven and bake for 8–10 minutes, or until the wreaths are lightly browned around the edges. Use pot holders to remove the pan from the oven.
6. Use a spatula to move the wreaths from the baking sheet to a cooling rack. Top each wreath with a cherry. Serve warm or at room temperature.

PER SERVING

Calories: 150 | Fat: 6g | Sodium: 220mg | Carbohydrates: 22g | Fiber: 0g | Sugar: 9g | Protein: 3g

Food Coloring

Liquid food coloring usually comes in red, blue, green, and yellow. Try mixing colors to make new colors. Red and yellow will make orange. Red and blue become purple. Be creative and try making your own interesting colors.

Could You Beat Molly?

Molly Schuyler set a world record in 2018—she ate 501 chicken wings in 30 minutes. That's more than sixteen wings per minute.

PARTY CHICKEN WINGS

DIFFICULTY:
MEDIUM

Everyone's favorite party snack is easy to make at home. If you have any leftovers, wrap them up for your lunch box—they taste great cold.

SERVES 5

1½ pounds chicken wings or drumettes

1½ teaspoons chili powder

1 teaspoon paprika

1 teaspoon ground cumin

½ teaspoon dried oregano

¼ teaspoon garlic powder

¼ teaspoon onion powder

½ cup blue cheese salad dressing

1. Preheat the oven to 450°F. Line a baking sheet pan with foil. Spray the foil with nonstick cooking spray.

2. Place the chicken wings in a large zip-top bag. Combine the chili powder, paprika, cumin, oregano, garlic powder, and onion powder in a small bowl. Pour the spices into the bag with the chicken. Seal the bag and shake it well to coat the chicken.

3. Remove the wings from the bag and place them on the baking sheet. Bake 35 minutes.

4. Reduce the heat to 375°F and bake another 20 minutes or until the chicken is browned. Turn off the oven and let the chicken sit in the oven for 20 minutes.

5. Use pot holders to remove the pan from the oven.

6. Serve the wings with the blue cheese dressing for dipping.

PER SERVING

Calories: 120 | Fat: 11g | Sodium: 290mg | Carbohydrates: 3g | Fiber: 1g | Sugar: 1g | Protein: 3g

drumette:

The meatier part of a chicken wing that looks like a small chicken leg drumstick.

NEW YEAR'S MOCKTAIL

For special events and family celebrations, it's fun to create a fancy "cocktail." Kids love having their own special drink. To make a fun drink stirrer, thread red and green grapes on a wooden skewer or toothpick.

SERVES 2

1 cup ice cubes

1 cup orange juice

1 cup lemonade

¼ cup grenadine syrup

1 unpeeled orange slice, cut in half

1. Fill two tall glasses with the ice.
2. Pour half of the orange juice and half of the lemonade into each of the glasses.
3. Very slowly, pour half of the grenadine into each glass.
4. Make a small cut halfway into the orange pieces. Place one piece on the rim of each glass.
5. Cheers!

PER SERVING

Calories: 190 | Fat: 0g | Sodium: 20mg | Carbohydrates: 48g | Fiber: 0g | Sugar: 44g | Protein: 1g

grenadine:

A cherry-flavored syrup used to make various cocktails that adds a little sweet-tart flavor and turns them pink.

Glossary

A

appetizer
a food or drink that stimulates the appetite and is usually served before a meal

B

bake
to cook something inside an oven

baking pan
a square or rectangular pan (glass or metal) used for baking and cooking food in the oven

baking sheet (also called cookie sheet or sheet pan)
a flat metal sheet used for baking cookies or other nonrunny items

baking spatula
a utensil with a wide plastic or silicone blade used to fold foods together or scrape down batter from mixing bowls

batter
a mixture made from ingredients like sugar, eggs, flour, and water that is used to make cakes, cookies, and pancakes

beat
to mix hard and thoroughly with a spoon, fork, whisk, or electric mixer

blend
to mix foods together until smooth

blender
an electric appliance used for blending liquids and grinding food

boil
to cook in a liquid until bubbles appear or until a liquid reaches its boiling point (water boils at 212°F/100°C)

broil
to put food under the broiler part of the oven, where the heat source is on top of the food

brown
to cook at low to medium heat until foods turn brown

C

can opener
a tool, either manual or electric, designed to open cans

carbonation
occurs when carbon dioxide is dissolved in water, resulting in the "fizz" found in seltzer and soda

casserole dish
a glass dish, usually a 1-quart or 2-quart size, used to make casseroles or baked goods in the oven

chill
to refrigerate food until it is cold

chop
to cut food into small pieces with a knife, blender, or food processor

colander
a metal or plastic bowl with holes in it used to drain water or liquids from foods such as pasta or vegetables

concentrate
a dense or strong liquid that had has some of the water removed from it

cool
to let food sit at room temperature until it is no longer hot

cooling rack
a wire rack on which hot food is placed, allowing air to circulate all around the items

craving
a great desire, taste, or hunger for a certain food or beverage

cream
to mix ingredients like sugar, butter, and eggs together until they are smooth and creamy

cutting board
a board made from wood or hard plastic used when slicing or chopping ingredients

D

dice
to chop food into small, even-sized square pieces

divided
when this word follows an item in the ingredients list of a recipe, it means that the listed amount of the ingredient is not used all at once; the ingredient will be needed in more than one step of the recipe

drain
to pour off a liquid in which the food has been cooked or stored

drizzle
to sprinkle drops of liquid, like chocolate syrup or an icing, lightly over the top of something, like cookies or a cake

drumette
the meatier part of a chicken wing that looks like a small chicken leg drumstick

Dutch oven
a large, heavy pot with a tight-fitting domed cover good for making large quantities of soup, chili, and pasta

E

electric mixer
an electric appliance used for mixing ingredients (like cake batter) together

F

fine-mesh strainer
a strainer with very small holes that can be used to strain or rinse foods that are very small, like quinoa or rice

fold
to gently combine ingredients together from top to bottom until they are just mixed together

G

grate
to shred food into tiny pieces with a grater, blender, or food processor

grease
to rub a baking pan or a dish with butter, vegetable shortening, or oil (or spray it with nonstick cooking spray) so food cooked on it won't stick

grenadine
a cherry-flavored syrup used to make various cocktails that adds a little sweet-tart flavor and turns them pink

H

hummus
a Middle Eastern dish that is a mixture of mashed chickpeas, garlic, and other ingredients, used especially as a dip for pita bread

I

ice cream scoop
a plastic or metal tool, shaped like a big spoon, used to scoop ice cream from a carton

K

kitchen shears
scissors for the kitchen that can be used to cut herbs and other foods

knead
to fold, press, and turn dough to make it the right consistency

knife
a tool with a sharp blade and a handle used to slice or chop foods

L

ladle
a large cup-shaped spoon with a long handle used to serve soup, stew, or chili

liquid measuring cup
a glass or plastic cup, used to measure liquids, with various measurements printed along the side

M

marinate
to soak meat, fish, or other foods in a liquid mixture before cooking; the liquid adds flavor to the food and sometimes makes the food (usually meats) more tender

mash
to crush food, like cooked potatoes, into a soft mixture

measuring cups
plastic or metal cups in different sizes used to measure dry ingredients, like sugar or flour

measuring spoons
plastic or metal spoons in different sizes used to measure small amounts of both liquid and dry ingredients

microwave oven
a small oven that heats food very quickly by cooking with electromagnetic waves (microwaves)

mince
to cut food into very small pieces

mix
to stir two or more ingredients together until they are evenly combined

mixing bowls
bowls (in various sizes) in which you mix ingredients together

molasses
the thick brown syrup that is separated from raw sugar during the refining process

muffin tin
a metal or glass pan with small round cups used for baking muffins and cupcakes

O

oven
a kitchen appliance for baking or broiling food

P

parfait glass
a special glass used to serve parfaits; it usually has a wide mouth and a narrower bottom

paring knife
a knife with a small blade, used to peel or cut small foods

pastry brush
a small brush used to spread melted butter or sauces over food

pitted
without the center pit (as in peaches, olives, or avocados)

pizza cutter
a tool with a rolling cutter used to easily cut pizzas, doughs, or flatbreads

plate
a flat dish used to serve food

potato masher
a tool used to mash cooked potatoes—or anything soft—to make them smooth

pot holders/oven mitts
pads or mittens used to hold hot pots, pans, baking sheets, and plates

powdered sugar
finely ground granulated sugar with cornstarch added; sometimes called confectioners' sugar

preheat
to turn an oven on and let it heat up before putting the food inside

purée
to mix in a blender or food processor until food is smooth and has the consistency of applesauce or a milkshake

Q

quinoa
the seed of a South American flowering plant; it is called a superfood because it's high in protein and other nutrients

R

ripe
fully developed and ready to be eaten

rolling pin
a wooden or plastic roller used to flatten an item such as dough for a piecrust

S

saucepan
a pot with a projecting handle used for stovetop cooking

sauté
to cook food on the stovetop in a skillet with a little liquid or oil

serving spoon
a large spoon used to scoop out portions of food

simmer
to cook over low heat while the food almost boils

skillet
a pan used for frying, stir-frying, and sautéing food in hot fat or oil

slice
to cut food into even-sized thin pieces

slotted spoon
a large spoon with holes in it to let liquid pass through

steam
to put food over a pan of boiling water so the steam can cook it

stir
to continuously mix food with a spoon

stir-fry
to cook food on the stovetop in a very hot pan while stirring constantly

stove
a kitchen appliance with gas or electric burners used for cooking food (also called a range or cooktop)

T

toast
to brown the surface of a food by heating

toaster oven
a small oven that sits on the kitchen counter used to toast, bake, or broil a small amount of food

tongs
a tool used to grasp, move, flip, and sear food, with two long arms joined at one end

tortilla
a round, flat, thin bread made with cornmeal or wheat flour that is commonly eaten with a topping or wrapped around a filling

turning spatula
a utensil with a wide, thin blade that is used to lift, turn, and flip foods like eggs, cookies, and hamburgers

W

whip
to beat rapidly with a whisk or an electric mixer

whisk
a utensil used for mixing and stirring liquid ingredients, like eggs and milk, together

wooden spoon
a big spoon made out of wood that is used for mixing and stirring just about any kind of food

Puzzle Answers

PAGE 13 • CRAZY COOKBOOKS

1000 PASTA DISHES, BY MACK A. RONEY
QUICK COOKING, BY MIKE ROE WAVE
YUMMY VEGETABLES, BY BROCK O'LEIGH
MEXICAN MEALS, BY AUNT CHILADA
LOSE WEIGHT!, BY CAL O. REEZE

PAGE 14 • YUMMY!

A. **Lettuce tossed with dressing**
   SALAD

B. **Melted rock from a volcano**
   LAVA

C. **Sound that bounces back**
   ECHO

D. **Back edge of the foot** HEEL

E. **An adult boy** MAN

F. **A baby bear** CUB

G. **A female deer** DOE

SO HE COULD HAVE A BALANCED MEAL

PAGE 16 • MEASURING SPOON MATH

FLOUR = 32 TBSP.
SUGAR = 24 TBSP.
COCOA = 4 TBSP.

PAGE 20 • A TASTY PUZZLE

WATER
SHORTENING
SOE
NUTRIENTS
ERE U U
Y E T G
LABELS A
T R

BUNCHES OF BAGELS

Page 23 • Bagel #1 is topped with PEANUT BUTTER
Page 25 • Bagel #2 is topped with HUMMUS
Page 31 • Bagel #3 is topped with CREAM CHEESE
Page 36 • Bagel #4 is topped with EGG SALAD
Page 39 • Bagel #5 is topped with GRAPE JELLY

PAGE 40 • BREAKFAST SCRAMBLES

What does a centipede have for breakfast?
BACON and LEGS
What does a lighthouse keeper have for breakfast?
BEACON and EGGS
What does a spook have for breakfast?
GHOST TOAST

PAGE 40 • WHAT'S SO FUNNY

The secret to "Cooktalk" is to add the word "EGG"
after every letter. When you remove all the extra EGGs,
here is the riddle that remains:
What two things can't you have for breakfast?
Lunch and dinner!

PAGE 45 • SILLY SLICE

ONE IS EASY TO
CHEAT, AND THE
OTHER IS CHEESY
TO EAT!

PAGE 54 • THE SOUP POT

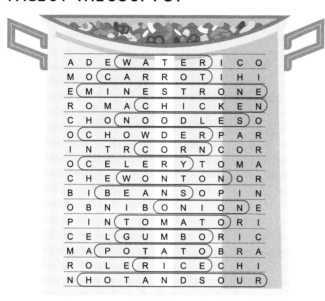

PAGE 56 • LUNCH?

A peanut butter and jellyfish sandwich!

PAGE 63 • CHIPS AND DIP

PAGE 64 • SORTING THE SNACKS

There are eight different kinds of snacks.

There is only one cheese puff. There are sixteen kernels of popcorn and only fifteen jelly beans.

PAGE 70 • LEFTOVERS

CUP CAKE
STRAW BERRY
POTATO SALAD
PEANUT BUTTER
POP CORN
CORN CHIPS
COLE SLAW

HOT DOG
HAM BURGER
FRENCH FRIES
TUNA MELT
APPLE SAUCE
EGG ROLL

PAGE 83 • OODLES OF NOODLES

PAGE 90 • CHEF ANDREW

Baked Beans, Cole Slaw, Rolls, Chicken Fingers, Iced Tea

PAGE 90 • KISS THE COOK

PAGE 94 • HIDDEN VEGGIES

ChoP EAch carrot very carefully!

ABE ANswered, "I love lettuce!"

Can you SPIN A CHerry?

Fill the CAB! BAG Each vegetable!

The BEE Tasted the broccoli.

PAGE 96 • SURPRISE SALAD

PAGE 114 • CUT THE CAKE

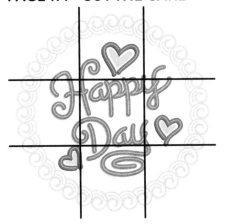

PAGE 121 • JIMMY LIKES...

Jimmy only likes vegetables that have double letters in them!

PAGE 126 • YOU SCREAM, I SCREAM

PAGE 129 • DRINK UP!

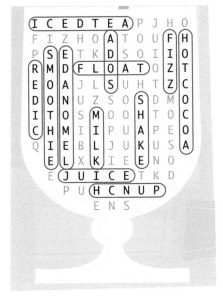

PAGE 131 • SEEING STARS

WHY DIDN'T THE ORANGE CROSS THE ROAD? IT RAN OUT OF JUICE!

PAGE 134 • I'M THIRSTY

1. MILK (Code is a simple number substitution, 1=A, 2=B, etc.)
2. SODA (Word is turned upside down and backward.)
3. SHAKE (Word is represented by a picture of a person shaking.)
4. WATER (H_2O is the chemical formula for water.)
5. JUICE (For each letter in the word, substitute the letter before it in the alphabet.)
6. ICED TEA (Drink is represented by a picture of the letter "T" with icicles hanging on it.)

PAGE 138 • WHO IS IT?

PAGE 143 • COOKIES

1. Wa**F**fle
2. P**U**dding
3. Noo**D**les
4. E**G**groll
5. Fri**E**s

PAGE 146 • IN THE KITCHEN

PAGE 148 • THE SILLY ANSWER IS, "IT WAS A TOTAL FLOP!"

APPLE   DROP   HOW   EAT

CHOP   DID   POMEGRANATE   SHOP

BET   POP   CHERRY   YOUR

PINEAPPLE   HEN   CROP   STRAWBERRY

MOP   UPSIDE DOWN   TOE   CAKE

HOP   STOP   TURN   TOP

OUT   HEW   RASPBERRY   WET

Recipe Index

My Recipes

Recipe Title: _____

Serves: _____

Ingredients

_____   _____

_____   _____

_____   _____

_____   _____

Directions

_____

_____

_____

_____

_____

_____

_____

Notes: _____

_____

My Recipes

Recipe Title: _____

Serves: _____

Ingredients

_____   _____

_____   _____

_____   _____

_____   _____

Directions

_____

_____

_____

_____

_____

_____

Notes: _____

_____

My Recipes

Recipe Title: _____

Serves: _____

Ingredients

_____   _____

_____   _____

_____   _____

_____   _____

Directions

_____

_____

_____

_____

_____

_____

_____

Notes: _____

_____

Draw Your Favorite Foods!

I Made These Recipes

RECIPE NAME	DATE	RATING	NOTES

Wind your way through pages of endless fun with

EVERYTHING® KIDS'!

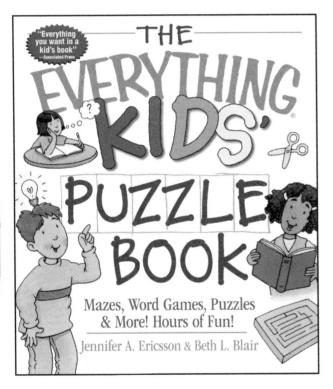

"Everything you want in a kid's book" —Associated Press

THE EVERYTHING KIDS' PUZZLE BOOK

Mazes, Word Games, Puzzles & More! Hours of Fun!

Jennifer A. Ericsson & Beth L. Blair

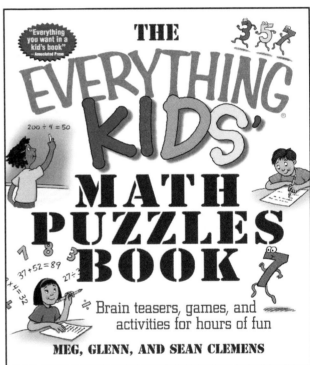

"Everything you want in a kid's book" —Associated Press

THE EVERYTHING KIDS' MATH PUZZLES BOOK

$200 \div 4 = 50$
$37 + 52 = 89$

Brain teasers, games, and activities for hours of fun

MEG, GLENN, AND SEAN CLEMENS

PICK UP OR DOWNLOAD YOUR COPIES TODAY!

adamsmedia
An Imprint of Simon & Schuster
A ViacomCBS COMPANY